PIVOTAL SWING

PIVOTAL SWING

How to Fundamentally Improve the Game of Baseball

(USING SIX SIGMA)

ROGER HART

TATE PUBLISHING
AND ENTERPRISES, LLC

Pivotal Swing
Copyright © 2012 by Roger Hart. All rights reserved.

No part of this publication may be reproduced, stored in a retrieval system or transmitted in any way by any means, electronic, mechanical, photocopy, recording or otherwise without the prior permission of the author except as provided by USA copyright law.

The opinions expressed by the author are not necessarily those of Tate Publishing, LLC.

Published by Tate Publishing & Enterprises, LLC
127 E. Trade Center Terrace | Mustang, Oklahoma 73064 USA
1.888.361.9473 | www.tatepublishing.com

Tate Publishing is committed to excellence in the publishing industry. The company reflects the philosophy established by the founders, based on Psalm 68:11,
"The Lord gave the word and great was the company of those who published it."

Book design copyright © 2012 by Tate Publishing, LLC. All rights reserved.
Cover design by Lauro Talibong
Interior design by Nathan Harmony

Published in the United States of America

ISBN: 978-1-62295-268-7
Sports & Recreation / Baseball
12.10.17

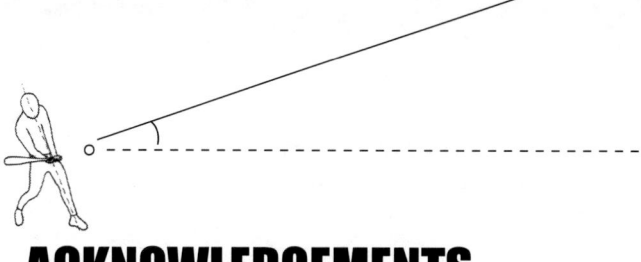

ACKNOWLEDGEMENTS

There are many people to whom I owe a great debt of gratitude for their contributions to this endeavor. I'm reasonably human and will probably not list all that deserve acknowledgement and thanks for their help over the years. More specifically (in no specific order):

Johnnie T. Dennis—National Teacher of the Year (for entire USA) in 1970 and my teacher for advanced math and physics (prep for college engineering). A true inspiration to all of us!

Air Academy Associates—Dr. Mark Kiemele and the whole team are truly inspirational leaders of process improvement through Six Sigma

Michael del Castillo—inspiration, help (lots) with the 'writing process' and editing

Rey Huerta—Sony executive, mentor and fellow enthusiast for process improvement and how to apply it

Keito Nakazawa—Sony executive and mentor

Tei Iki–Sony executive and mentor

Sei Tanaka—Sony executive and linkage to Six Sigma acceptance in Sony Corp. (Japan)

Col. Gordon Brown, Albert Almuete—Sony Master Blackbelts for training and utilization of Six Sigma (more importantly—process improvement)

Tony Lim–Sony manager/Blackbelt and part of the Six Sigma Deployment Team

Bill Townsend—Sony Engineer/Greenbelt and fellow enthusiast for process improvement application to the game of baseball

William 'Bill' Bieloh—High School baseball and leadership coach

Coleman (Fred) Butler—fellow technician of the swing process, good friend and confidant

Mykl Clason—fellow engineer with application to math and physics

Kevin Buchmueller, Chris Pratt, Rick Reynolds, Gery Katona, Matts Olssen and Jeff Anstett—close friends with huge levels of patience to hear me rant about this over the years

Kevin Hart—my son and official motivation to pursue analysis of the hitting process; he's been a 'trouper' as we worked on it over the years; he also did the drawings

Roxanne Hart—my lovely, patient & forgiving wife and confidant. (Emphasis on patient!)

Keri Hart, John Hart, Amy Hart-Ives, Sherry Lorang—family, though not directly involved, have had to endure my arduous development & long writing processes

Last and most importantly, my Lord and savior Jesus Christ—maybe someday I'll learn why he chose me to develop & introduce this process.

CONTENTS

Key Points & Objectives 11

Foreword by Mark J. Kiemele, Ph.D. 15

Preface 23

Introduction 27

1st INNING
Change? No way! Vs. We Have To! 33

2nd INNING
The Five Axioms of the Pivotal Swing® 49

3rd INNING
What is Process Improvement All About? 63

4th INNING
Is Hitting an Art or a Science? 83

5th INNING
The Hitting Process—Inputs & Outputs. 87

6th INNING
Getting Started on Improvements 113

7th INNING
Focus on Additional Improvements. 133

8th INNING
Dramatic Test Results 159

9th INNING
Who Will Benefit the Most? 167

10th INNING
What Is the Impact on the Game?. 181

11th INNING
Clarification of the Pivotal Swing® method 201

12th INNING
How Does Intellectual Property Fit Into this Picture? 221

END NOTES 227

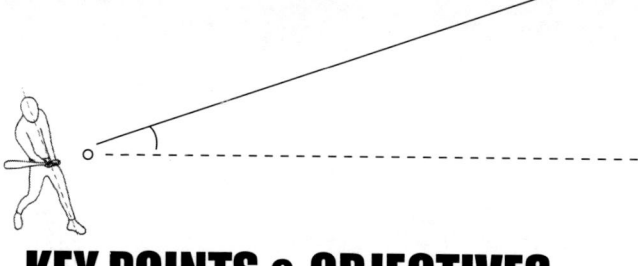

KEY POINTS & OBJECTIVES

This book is of interest to anyone that likes the game of baseball and fast-pitch softball. If you are a player, it will help you. If you are a parent, grandparent, family member or friend of a player, you can be part of helping that player improve their hitting. If you are a 'fan' of the game, you will never see the game as before.

Billy Beane in 'Moneyball' used statistics (a scientific method) to change the management perspective of team member selection. Yes, a scientific method changed the game of baseball! This book is about using scientific (Six Sigma–process improvement) methods to improve the hitting process. That is *equivalent to 'Moneyball' on steroids* and, it too, will change the game of baseball!

More than 80% of Fortune 100 and 50% of Fortune 500 companies have used Six Sigma methods for improving their wide diversity of business processes. (iSixSigma Magazine)

There hasn't been a .400 hitter in MLB since 1941 (Ted Williams–more than 70 years ago)?

Ted Williams is renowned for his statement: "Hitting is the most difficult thing to do in sports."

There hasn't been any *significant* improvement in the hitting process in the last 50 years?

We show you how to improve the swing process that has to be executed in 0.2 seconds?

Nobody has ever clearly shown the most important OUTPUT of the hitting process. We do! (Hint—not base hits, home-runs or power)

We show you how to reduce the time to execute the swing. A 0.04 second reduction in the swing process gives a 20% improvement in the time the hitter has to decide whether to hit that pitch. 20%–that is a huge benefit!

Revealed: the #1 cause of swing 'inaccuracy'!

During the last 25 years in MLB (both NL & AL) the average difference between the top and bottom team's batting average is less than 34 points! That is why an improved process will change the game of baseball!

We produced a 30% improvement in the primary hitting 'Output'! That % may not correlate directly to batting average. If it does, that converts a .240 batting average to .312. That would 'fundamentally change the game of baseball'!

Prediction—The Pivotal Swing® method is so solid in the fundamentals and improvement that the Little League (LL) team that implements it best, will win the next LL World Series.

Imagine–a high school physics teacher could inspire 'changing the game of baseball'!

If you are looking for a "Competitive Advantage"—this is it!

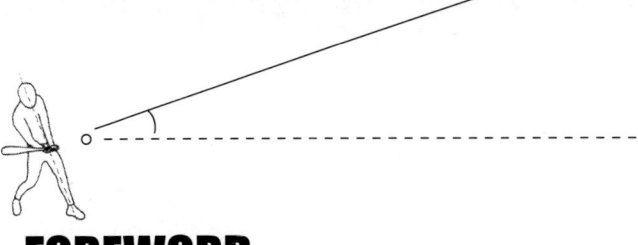

FOREWORD
by Mark J. Kiemele, Ph.D.

This book is about change! And the context is baseball, more specifically, the "hitting" process. Roger Hart has done a masterful job of blending the art and science of hitting by developing a robust design methodology that will impact the game of baseball forever. That is a strong statement, because baseball is the American Pastime, the game that brings to the fans solace, meaning, and hope (at least in the springtime). Caution: if you read this book, you will never think about hitting the same way ever again. Legitimate, positive change in any endeavor is not possible without process improvement methods. This book provides an actionable process improvement methodology that, if applied according to the detailed instructions presented, will result in improved hitting performance. Even if you have never played the game of baseball, this book will provide insight into how you can go about improving any aspect of your life.

Process improvement has become a key competitive advantage in almost every aspect of business, government, and academia. Without it, change is not possible. Can process improvement be learned or is it innate? The advent and propagation of Six Sigma over the last 20 years as a process improvement vehicle has proven its worth in almost every industry imaginable. Research documented in iSixSigma Magazine shows that more than 80% of the Fortune 100 companies and more than 50% of the Fortune 500 companies have used Six Sigma to make the necessary improvements to become or remain competitive in the marketplace. Six Sigma is the option of choice when it comes to improving the key performance metrics that guide our businesses, because it is the best methodology available today. While some companies deploy Six Sigma better than others, the fact remains that Six Sigma is a proven, reliable, and predictable means of improving performance. The amazing property of Six Sigma is that anyone can learn it and apply it. Unfortunately, very few do. Fortunately, Roger Hart's success as the Director of Six Sigma Deployment at Sony Electronics shines through in this book, as he has worked more than a decade on applying the principles of Six Sigma to the hitting process. And the result is that he has made some impressive analytical breakthroughs or core level process improvements, as he calls them.

Six Sigma is a process improvement engine, a powerful driver that targets the very nature of why processes fail: variation. Variation in performance is the equivalent of terrorism in societies. It creates havoc in our processes. Any activity that has inputs (variables that affect performance) and outputs (performance measures) is a process. And all inputs and outputs exhibit variation. Variation in the inputs creates variation in the outputs. Thus, if we can control or remove variation in the variables or factors that impact our performance, we will be able to achieve substantial improvement in the measurable outputs. Identifying, understanding, removing, and controlling variation in any process is the key to success. Six Sigma is about getting at the right measures as outputs and then finding the key input factors that affect those measures. Roger has done an impeccable job of breaking the entire "hitting" process into smaller chunks (or sub-processes) where he has shown the linkage of measurable outputs from one sub-process being inputs to the next sub-process, and so on. This is a key Six Sigma property that brings superb value to the analysis process.

One industry where the application of Six Sigma has been noticeably absent is in professional sports. Considering the money that is spent in the professional sports industry, it is amazing that owners and franchise operators do not demand more for their money. The recent movie, Moneyball, documents the desire and success of the Oakland Athletics to achieve playoff status at a much lower investment than their competitors invest. In fact, it took an outsider to convince Billy Beane, the GM of the A's, to use other metrics, like On-Base-Percentage (OBP), to get better performance at lower cost. The OBP metric was used primarily to bring in the appropriate lower-paid players who will produce more runs. But the movie did not show how to improve OBP. That is the next step and that is what this book is about. How can we bring "all players" to a higher level of performance? If we could improve the batting average of "all players," then we could not only improve their OBP, which is known to produce more runs, but change the very nature of the game itself. If we were to achieve even a 5% improvement in batting average, e.g., a .260 hitter moves to .273, a .280 hitter moves to .294, and a .300 hitter moves to .315, the OBP would increase dramatically. Statistical analysis by way of Six Sigma can show the impact this batting average improvement can have on run production and, ultimately, playoff opportunities. While batting average is the measure of hitting we are exposed to daily, this book delves into the critical factors that impact batting average, and then drills down even further, getting to the factors that affect those factors. The process of hitting can be broken down into smaller pieces, each of which has inputs and outputs, just like any other process. Perhaps some of the inputs to the hitting process might be: time until batter determines the pitch to be a fast ball, slider, or curve ball; the length of the bat; the weight of the bat; the stance taken in the batter's box; etc. Just like any other process, hitting has a lot of factors associated with it that will impact its performance measures such as batting average or OBP.

This book does a remarkable job of analyzing the "hitting" process and doing so in a very simple manner that anyone can understand. It emphasizes getting the "right" data, namely measuring the "right" things, because getting the "right" data will get the "right" knowledge which will enable the "right" kind of change. This book is the very first of its kind to apply the scientific methods of Six Sigma to improve a specific process in the sports industry, while still incorporating the advantages of good coaching into the entire improvement process.

There is no other sport that is inundated with so many statistics as baseball. It is not uncommon to hear during a World Series game, for example, that a batter is hitting .xxx against lefties with two outs and runners on 2nd and 3rd (with a 95% probability of heavy rain occurring in the next 2 minutes!). Unfortunately, these are all descriptive statistics and while presented to imply predictability, they have very little if any predictive power. We are all fooled at some point by random variation which, coincidentally, is the basis of many sports superstitions. What is needed is more of the discovery type of statistics. The nature of the latter type of statistics, which Six Sigma is adept at detecting, is to determine the critical factors or variables that impact performance. If we can discover these, as this book does for hitting, then we are on the path of improving those descriptive statistics such as batting average or OBP. Six Sigma is the study of variation in process inputs and process outputs and how the two are related. Once the relationships between inputs and outputs are established, then improvement across the entire spectrum of team members is possible.

The biggest hurdle that any organization faces in finding these relationships, professional sports included, is the culture of the organization. Most cultures already assume they know these relationships. Unfortunately, only the process truly knows those relationships, and we have to discover them. Six Sigma provides the means of discovery—through the detailed examination of the various process steps and associated data. Cultures also assume that their processes are different than others'. Of course they are. As the noted American anthropologist Margaret Mead once said, *"Always remember that you are absolutely unique, just like everyone else."* The fact of the matter remains that every process has inputs and outputs. Yes, the names of the inputs and outputs differ from industry to industry and from application to application, but the key is understanding the relationships between inputs and outputs. Once those relationships are established, variation reduction and robust performance in the presence of uncontrolled variation, as described in this book, will lead to unprecedented success.

Look out, baseball. If the robust design methodology presented in this book is implemented as described, it is very likely that we will see Ted Williams' .406 batting average in 1941 as the last .400 hitter and the unimaginable record of the 56-game hitting streak also set in 1941 by The Yankee Clipper, Joe DiMaggio, broken within the next 10 years. Both of these records have been deemed "unbreakable" by baseball experts. Not so. This book provides the recipe for changing the entire way baseball is played. All that remains is to just go do it.

—Mark J. Kiemele, Ph.D.
President and Co-founder
Air Academy Associates
www.airacad.com

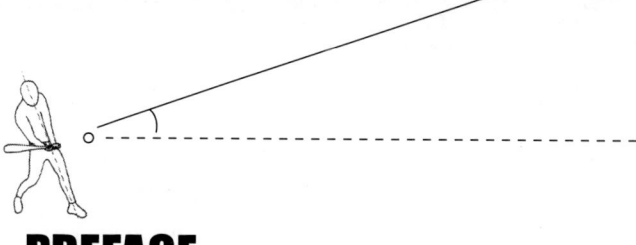

PREFACE

I used to think swinging a baseball bat was the most natural thing in the world. It was like climbing trees, or seeking out the feel of sunlight on my skin, or wishing I had my shoes off when I walked through a lawn of freshly cut grass. No one ever taught me these things, they just happened.

I couldn't remember the first time I held a bat, or climbed a tree or craned my neck to feel the sun on my face, or felt the feel of grass in between my toes, they were just things that had always been—things I had always done.

But swinging a bat isn't natural at all. It was taught to me by my father during a time in my childhood before I was even forming memories. The baseball swing may be art, it may be science, but either way it is a process of human invention, and like all processes, can be improved.

The thing is, the baseball swing itself is kind of ancient. Versions of the game have been traced back as far as the 14th century, though I imagine even before humanity had fashioned a stick into its first spear, it had used a club for survival. Early forms of man had developed a swing and hit a lot of things with their club (bat) long before considering it for recreation. Though an invention it is, it is possibly one of the oldest inventions of human kind.

And so it was, in those primitive times, which the process of the swing evolved over time—like language, or math, or art—and in that sense, yes, it is natural.

But like all processes in recent time—language, art and math included—since the dawn of the industrial era the speed of improvement has been increasing, and occasionally, a giant leap in progress is made.

The application of management practices developed in high-tech factories around the world, and refined over years through hundreds of thousands of applications, allows us to stand on the shoulders of great thinkers, and instead of starting a fresh with each process improvement, start where they left off—though on a new improvement.

The book you are holding is the product of first and foremost my love of baseball. About that I want to be perfectly clear. But it is also the product of generations of thinkers who have solved problems as immense as an international station floating in space, and as tiny as a micro-processor (computer chip). And it is the product of my life's commitment to learning from these great thinkers, and teaching their lessons to the next generation.

Through the course of reading this book you will experience a bit of my personal journey as I moved from playing little league in Walla Walla, to implementing a $10 million project at Sony, to teaching my own son how to swing a bat, and for the first time questioning what it was my own father had taught me, and his father him.

And at the end, with the process dissected, simplified and reassembled, we will all come out in a new era of baseball: rebirth of the .400 hitter.

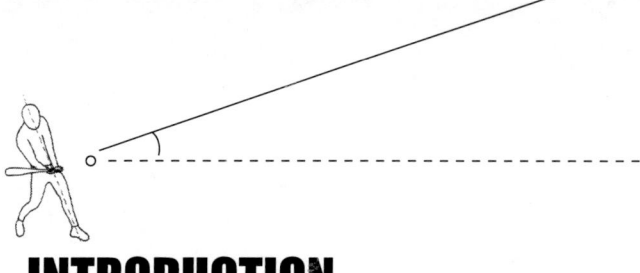

INTRODUCTION

I hope you didn't pick this title (book) looking for a novel or casual read. If so, you will be very disappointed. This book is not for casual readers. This book is about the science of baseball and it will test your ability to absorb new knowledge and challenge you to become part of a new era of .400 hitters in MLB.

Who in their right mind would consider fundamentally changing baseball? Yes, it is a bold claim. Not so big an issue when thought of in terms of process improvement methods and 'change' management.

Long ago many thought it impossible to put a man on the moon (let alone bring him home safely). I suppose they view it a lot differently now as compared to 50 years ago. Why? Although our answers might differ somewhat in the words, the concept or content will be essentially the same. The reason is: it has been done. A more explicit version of that is: hindsight is much, much, much easier that foresight. However, if we break down any huge endeavor into smaller pieces, it will be easier for anyone to assess it.

A major contributor to why the 'naysayers' didn't think a lunar landing was possible is they didn't have the same knowledge as those that believed it possible. I may be going out on a limb here but I seriously doubt that you, I and vast numbers of other folks had the knowledge of the scientists, engineers and project managers that believed they could achieve a lunar landing. This exemplifies why some folks don't believe something can be achieved when others with specific knowledge do.

I'm not the next Walter Alston or Joe Torre, I'm just a serious fan who watched (and played) a lot of baseball and through the scientific method discovered an opportunity for batters to dramatically improve their averages. I came to view pitching duels such as the famous Marichial/Spahn duel of 1963—when each pitcher faced more than 50 batters—not as an achievement of great pitching, but as a failure of hitting.

The scientific method has been successfully applied to almost every aspect of our lives, from automobile production to startup businesses, and as Billy Beane's A's have demonstrated, it can also be applied to the game of baseball. The Pivotal Swing® is the result of my application of exactly such analytical thinking and it will redefine the relationship between pitchers and batters. It is the goal of this book to not only demonstrate that the .400 hitter revolution is possible, but also to give a blueprint for how we will make it happen.

Do You Have an Attitude for Change?

Some folks accept change easily; others actually lead the process of change. New knowledge is usually the first impetus to change. With new and additional knowledge most of us have changed different aspects of our lives. Think about it! Think back over your life at the various changes you have gone through and reflect upon how new and additional knowledge was a part of that process.

I will venture to say that any huge or complicated matter is much harder to view in its entirety than if it were broken down into smaller pieces. Let's get back to the moon issue. Did we have rocket technology? Did we know how to provide food and drink to someone in extended travel? Did we know how to provide air (oxygen) to someone in a place where there is none? I could go on, but you see my point. If we break the big endeavor down into small pieces and then assess the individual pieces, it is much easier to reach a bold conclusion than if we look only at the large endeavor.

Building on that view, I'm willing to bet that you personally have at some time in your life, taken on a big project. More than likely you didn't just blast out and do it. It is much more likely that you assessed it, made plans, broke the big project down into pieces and then (and only then) did you actually start to achieve the big project or objective. I won't take away that there are a few that didn't break it down into pieces. And, I suspect that there were a lot more successes from those who did. Many of you can relate to the famous quote by the Chinese philosopher Lao Tzu that begins with, "A journey of a thousand miles …" You may have even received it in a fortune cookie if you eat Chinese food regularly. Most of us view that walking for a thousand miles is a huge endeavor. However, many have done it. As I claimed earlier, I suspect those that did are ones that broke it into pieces and mapped it from one city to the next. They made provisions and studied to gain new knowledge of where they were heading. They then implemented their plan one segment at a time.

What is the ending to Lao Tzu's famous quote? It is, "A journey of a thousand miles begins with a single step."

You may realize as did I that there are two meanings to this quote. Here are my views. From a knowledge standpoint the 'beginning with a single step' is to make the plan. It is to organize and get ready, study, plan and gain new knowledge to prepare for the huge endeavor. The second meaning is from a 'will' to do it standpoint. If you don't actually take the first step you can't achieve the final goal. After you have prepared, your will must compel you to move, take a single step. I'll venture to say that Lao-tzu had at least these two views in mind. There is a good chance he had even more in mind. Those two views are sufficient to help us with this book.

I will show you the new knowledge on 'HOW' to improve the hitting process and achieve the objectives of this book. It is up to 'YOU' and those who have the 'WILL' to use it. Unused knowledge is an immense waste. I firmly believe there are a large number of very special individuals out there that will embrace this new knowledge and lead us into the new era!!

"Wise men store up knowledge …."

Proverbs 10:14

Let's get this ball game started!

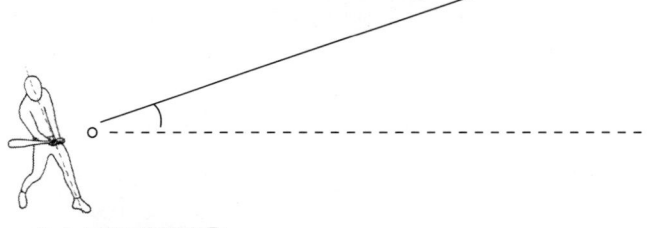

1st INNING
Change?
No way! Vs. We Have To!

What the heck! Why not boldly state what this book is about? The title (sub-title) alludes to it in multiple ways. The Pivotal Swing® (registered trademark) not only describes a new swing for the game of baseball, fast-pitch softball, and similar sports. It also identifies what it will do in the game of baseball. It will take the whole book to build the knowledge on *What*, *Why* and *How* that statement can be made. Whether you are a player, a player's father/mother, a coach or anyone else involved with hitting or helping others be better hitters, this book is going to change the dimensions of and how you view the process of hitting. Is it going to be easy? I am pretty sure it will not. You might be surprised at why I am a little pessimistic as we venture into explaining what is involved.

That comes from my extensive experience in dealing with change in the corporate world. We have all had to deal with change in our personal lives, jobs and businesses. However, we typically are not consciously focused on the issue of change. We tend to focus on what we have to do to adapt because of other changes that have taken place in products and processes.

I don't think the elements or the execution of the new swing will be anywhere near as complicated as dealing with the change in attitude needed to achieve it. As both a process improvement specialist and strategic developer I learned that oftentimes, changing long-term and well-established beliefs is more complicated than changing actions.

Every person that reads this book will do so for a different reason. Some folks will want to bypass the process of development and jump to the conclusions. That isn't wise. Every idea is connected to every other idea, and to fully understand the Pivotal Swing®, one must understand the context in which it was developed. Not knowing how to approach a strategic change or why decisions were made only leads to misunderstanding. Skipping steps messes with more than just depth of understanding, it messes with the batter's confidence.

Without understanding the information that went into the development of the Pivotal Swing® the batter will miss out on half its benefits and lack the skills to fully implement the full range of what it offers.

Whatever you do don't jump to the end thinking that some single technique will change the way you hit. To do so is to miss out on the important lessons to be learned through the process of building new knowledge, and will render you defenseless in the psychological warfare of finding, learning and implementing your own version of this technique.

Change Is Common to All of Us

We have all dealt with changes in our personal lives—some forced, and others chosen. Think puberty, aging, and accidents leading to comas, all of which affect change beyond our control. And yet, for our purposes, let us set aside such involuntary or biological changes and instead take a look at changes based upon knowledge or beliefs and identify a few where the transformation is a decision.

The search for transformative experiences is often instigated by circumstances beyond our control. Being diagnosed with a disease may lead us to read a book about its causes and ways to mitigate its effects. Or the death of a loved one may cause us to reevaluate our religious beliefs, and the way we live our life. The changes may be designed to reduce pain, prevent others from getting the same disease, save your life, or the life of a loved one.

Regardless of why the change is instigated there are specialists with in-depth knowledge to guide or influence our choices. And yet even with such specialists as doctors, in spite of all their wisdom and experience, in the end, they can only advise, leaving the final decision to make a change to us—the amateurs.

In the case of the Pivotal Swing® the change is of this latter, knowledge-based type. No one is forcing us to change, and though it seems to have arisen naturally as an almost evolutionary process of baseball, it is not inevitable, and if the change is to be effected, both within your personal game, and within the game generally speaking, there is first some essential knowledge we must acquire.

Change Isn't Easy!

Getting back to my earlier point, expressing this new knowledge is much easier than changing the attitudes and long-term beliefs surrounding the hitting process—the Pivotal Swing® takes a stand against age old traditions, the status quo and much of the accepted baseball dogma. I hope that after you finish the book you look back with a sense that the process is easy to understand, and if I may be so bold, even a bit intuitive. However, the will and attitude to implement the process will be much more difficult.

Some transformations are easy. And in my opinion, once you have the will to implement the necessary changes, the Pivotal Swing® is very easy indeed. And yet those who have not read this book may simply not be willing to accept its tenants until they have seen the swing successfully implemented with their own eyes. But we must not be deterred by their doubt. We must remain logical and reasonable to the highest degree possible and recognize the early adopters of any process are always viewed as outliers or maybe crazies. But when they see the success with their own eyes, they too will want to be part of the group that started the revolution.

Many of the practices this book challenges have been implemented by some of baseball's most respected leaders for generations, and those practices remain in vogue because they work. They produce baseball players like Derek Jeter, Paul Molitor, Alex Rodriguez, Pete Rose and my favorite, Tony Gwynn, but they have failed to produce a Ted Williams since, well, Ted Williams. And as a former process improvement director at Sony I look at the game of baseball through wholly different eyes.

Sure, some of my fondest childhood memories are playing baseball. I played in the Pee-Wee League in Walla Walla, Washington during the (1960's); I was a decent high-school player and am proud to this day for being known as a clutch hitter during my late teens. One of the best memoires was participating as a fan when the Padres defeated the Cubs to win game 5 of the 1984 NLCS.

But I am no MLB player. I am a fan that has played a lot. I'm also a fan with a lot of process improvement knowledge and experience. That is a different class of fan.

My challenge is to convince you that although these players are talented, even my favorite, Tony Gwynn who holds a .338 lifetime batting average, mastered the game with guts and a lot of hard work, they were missing key information in their decision-making processes, and therefore, in the way they played the game. Yes, guts and hard work go a long, long way, and to be sure, in the case of baseball's greatest players and coaches, they have gone much further than I managed.

But the aim of this book is to show that working smarter along with hard work will get you further. Guts and hard work may be sufficient to turn a .250 hitter into a .300 hitter. However, new knowledge along with guts and hard work can turn that same player into a .350 hitter. The goal of this book is to help every hitter improve. A key point though is that without working smarter, there appears to be a limit. There has for decades been a management mantra to 'work smarter, not harder'. Why not work *smarter and harder* to get even better results. Though the .250 hitter that improves to a .300 or .330 hitter will be good, we also want to help the .330 hitter become the 1st .400 hitter in over 70 years. And for that, the new knowledge of the Pivotal Swing® is essential.

Does every nutritionist and doctor give the same dietary advice? Sure there'll be an overlap in philosophies, but there will be great divergence as well. The similarities that do exist will likely arise from common education and experience. Similarly, the differences will arise from the differing education and experience. The more diverse the education and experience, the more diverse the recommendations will be. And my education and experiences in process improvement brings an entirely different set of tools and perspectives to the assessment of hitting. Unique? No. Unique in a baseball fan who actually applied those tools to creating improvements? Absolutely!

In The Beginning ...

I did not set out to reinvent the baseball swing. And I certainly did not set out to create the first .400 hitter to play in the Majors in 70 years. I wish I could say I was so audacious, but in fact, it was a bit of circumstance, and a true love for the game that led to the writing of this book.

My most recent corporate career was dedicated to implementing a business management strategy known as Six Sigma—widely known and recognized as a way to improve processes or the way people do things, in any field. Six Sigma, a form of Process Improvement (PI), was 1st initiated by the late Bill Smith, who in 1986 convinced then–Chief Executive of Motorola, Robert Galvin that implementing the strategy would generate error-free products 99.99966% of the time, and to a large degree he was correct. By one account the technique for analyzing and improving processes has saved Motorola $15 billion over the past eleven years.

When the former Motorola executive Rick Schroeder transferred to Allied Signal in 1994, he brought with him his faith in the Six Sigma philosophy, implementing it at his new employer. Five years later Allied Signal was looking at $600 million in Six Sigma related savings every single year.

So successful was Six Sigma that in 1996 the former CEO of General Electric, Jack Welch committed to a full conversion of the company by 2000. Two years later, even before full implementation was in place, the Six Sigma effort was contributing $700 million in corporate benefits.

When I began in 1997 as the Director of Quality Systems at Sony we received $10 million to start deployment of the strategy and start training our members. I worked with key leadership at Sony to implement a full-blown Six Sigma Program in all Sony Electronics, Inc. operations, and I was completely convinced that any effective organization needed to know and fully utilize the process improvement (PI) tools and methods of a Six Sigma Program in all parts of their organization. Not too much later I became the Director of Six Sigma Deployment and we set out to develop, teach, implement and use Six Sigma process improvement tools in all our operations.

Three years later we had saved the company nearly $500 million.

So as my son began his Little League journey it was only natural for me to look at his swing through Six Sigma eyes. Slowly, over months the idea that Six Sigma process improvement could be applied to baseball began to grow into a fully developed philosophy. While deploying Six Sigma at Sony I began to share in various sessions that PI tools had noticeably improved my son's hitting. He made the all-star team. At that age there is a lot of variation and it wasn't clear if that achievement was his personal skill or the hitting method we were developing.

By sharing with my colleagues the successes of Six Sigma in such a diverse process as hitting a baseball, I hoped to demonstrate that PI tools can be applied to any process. Indeed it helped the managers and trainees alike to visualize and break-down mental barriers keeping them from accepting and applying those tools in their own business endeavors.

It wasn't until after I left Sony that I finally had the time to really dig into the data and videos I was accumulating. Slowly from careful analysis of thousands of swings something new started to coalesce that would impact the course of my future endeavors. Namely, that hitters are 'punished' for being close. I'll have to explain that later. The more I dug into the data and assessment the more developed became my sense of purpose. Finally, beyond anything I would have guessed at those first practices in the front yard of our home in San Diego, what I began to realize was that what my son and I had in fact been developing was an entirely new hitting process.

And I knew that if I found the proper context for the data, and pursued new data accordingly, the data itself would reveal what needed to be done to improve the hitting process. My new purpose became the need to find out why we hadn't had a .400 hitter in MLB in over 70 years and find some way to change it.

Examples of Improved Products & Processes

Can you think of any innovation in sports in the past 50 years that has totally changed the game? Humor me, and don't look ahead until you have taken a few minutes to give it a shot. Think in terms of products as well as processes and methods. Likely it will be harder than you to think, though you may surprise me or yourself and manage to list some.

When I did this, my list included the oversized tennis racket, alloy bats which are so revolutionary they aren't even allowed in the Majors, the compound bow for archery, new golf clubs such as drivers, parabolic snow skis, and snowboards.

Your list may have included others, but I doubt your list included many innovative methods, instead focusing as mine did initially on products. I think that is entirely natural. Most of us, when we think of great innovations, think of products, not processes. If your list did include a method or two it might be the one-handed free-throw shot (yes, I can remember when two-handed and granny-style shots were pervasive!) or the slam-dunk, football's transition from mostly a running game to mostly a passing game, and for the high-jump fans out there, there is the revolutionary Fosbury Flop.

Named after Dick Fosbury, who won the 1968 Olympic gold medal in the high-jump employing his method, the Flop supplanted the straddle technique, the Western Roll, the Eastern cutoff, and the Scissor-Jump to become the ubiquitous style employed by every elite jumper on the planet. Fosbury's Flop represents one of the most dramatic single method changes in sports in recent history and exemplifies what Six Sigma calls a 'core level' process improvement and permanently changed the way the sport is played.

Like products, only the fittest processes survive, and those which do not adapt will cease to be employed. For every human invention—whether product or process—if given enough time, eventually another, better invention will be developed, accepted and implemented—and make no mistake, baseball is no different.

Change? We have too!

Although I wish it were otherwise, I accept that there are folks who will argue that baseball is doing just fine the way it is—that there is no problem with no .400 hitters. And heck! They are entitled to an opinion.

I expect that every hitter in all of baseball would love to do better. Wanting to do better is radically different than pursuit of a quantum leap in performance.

Those that want to do significantly better should know Einstein's definition of Insanity. He defined, "Insanity—doing the same thing over and over again and expecting different results." He was a very smart guy. Using his wisdom, it is clear that we have to change. Trying to make changes without the right tools is extremely impractical.

Those of us that are serious about a major improvement in the hitting process will completely accept the need to change. Change without wisdom of how to choose the 'right' changes is folly. It is unrealistic to think that a current player or coach without training in process improvement tools, would be successful in such an endeavor. My background and experience match the needs of this challenge.

Those folks that are happy with the game as it is today shouldn't read this book or attempt the Pivotal Swing®. They are the traditional players or fans who remember the good ole days fondly and don't ever want them to change, and they are as much a part of the game as the old-time players themselves. I feel the same camaraderie with them that I do with all fans of baseball. However, players with this attitude are not the first adopters who will best be able to capitalize on this new technique and implement it to the detriment of all in the old, traditional guard. These are the players who will change last, and will change when they have no other choice than to do so.

2nd INNING
The Five Axioms of the Pivotal Swing®

1. Nobody in Major League Baseball (MLB) has hit over .400 since 1941 when Ted Williams hit .406.

2. Hitting is a process.

3. Any process, including the hitting process, can be improved.

4. Baseball is unique in that the hitter is *'punished'* for being close.

5. Break the Cycle–If you do what you have always done, you will get the same results you have always achieved. To dramatically improve the hitting process something has to change.

All the data gathered using practical Performance Improvement (PI) techniques have lead to several inarguable truths. And what those truths reveal is that the hitting process is ready for a major paradigm shift.

But first, let us understand the foundation of the Pivotal Swing® development.

Axiom #1—No .400 hitter in over 70 years

There has been no .400 hitter in MLB since Ted Williams hit .406 in 1941, over 70 years ago! Is that reflective of Ted William's renowned statement, "Hitting is the most difficult thing to do in sports"? Does that mean it is impossible? Absolutely not! Only people that don't want to challenge tradition would conclude otherwise. After seeing PI successfully applied in such diverse contexts as GE jet engine manufacturing, Bank of America operational processes, Motorola semiconductor chip development, GlaxoSmithKline pharmaceutical development, and Sony marketing & product development processes, it came as no surprise that the methods also work in baseball processes.

Axiom #2—Hitting is a Process

To many it is intuitive that hitting involves a combination of serial and parallel steps accomplished in a matter of a split second. That is a clear representation of a process. But others will argue, I am unnecessarily complicating the swing by calling it a process. To them it is just one thing, one movement, and cannot be broken down further. But there can be no Pivotal Swing®, without accepting this axiom at face value.

Axiom #3—Any Process Can Be Improved

Since we won't thoroughly review process improvement (PI) until the 3rd Inning, I must ask you to accept a much higher authority than I on this subject. If you read Dr. Kiemele's Foreword to the book, you have heard from the epitome of the experts on this subject. Not only was I his student, so have been the executives of many Fortune 500 companies. As an expert and an instructor of experts, he gave it to you straight: any process can be improved. Yes, including sports and baseball, specifically the hitting process. He, as well as all instructors at Air Academy Associates, LLP, teaches all students the foundation, concepts and most importantly the tools with which to achieve success at improving any process. You would have a very hard time conjuring up a process that they haven't taught someone how to improve it. And better yet, you leave the training with the motivation to get your _____ out there and 'do it'.

Axiom #4—Hitter is '*Punished*' for being close!

Be warned, we are now entering the world of science, math and physics. Not to say the material is so horribly complex that we can't understand it, but be prepared that we may have to work a bit harder.

We know that in the game of baseball, if a hitter swings and miss the ball they are given 1 strike against them. And they get 3 strikes before they lose the opportunity to swing any more. But what most don't realize, are some of the specific dimensions involved: the maximum diameter of the bat is 2 3/4 inches and a MLB sanctioned ball is 9 to 9 1/4 inches (229—235 mm) in circumference and 2 7/8—3 inches (73—76 mm) in diameter.

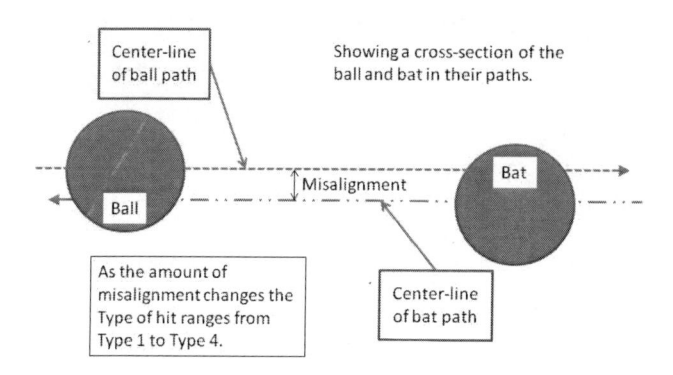

Diagram1 - Alignment: center-line of bat-to-ball

Let us assume the desired hit, or output, of a .400 hitter is a line-drive. We need to describe four types of hits, defined by sets of dimensions at which the ball makes contact with the bat. The first type, resulting in a line-drive exhibits a misalignment of +/- 3/8 inch, also known as the sweet-spot. Type 2 which might result in either a fly-ball or grounder exhibits a +/- 3/4 inch misalignment. Type 3 is most likely a foul-tip also resulting in a strike but with the benefit of not being an out on the 3rd strike, exhibits a +/- 1 1/2 inches misalignment. And yes, type 4 is the pure miss, exhibiting a misalignment of +/- 3 inches. Or, the proverbial, he/she 'fanned' on that one.

The results of, type 3 & 4 really aren't that much different other than the above noted 3rd strike divergence. Type 1 is what all successful hitters are trying to achieve. Which leaves Type 2? Hitters don't want Type 2s because they are typically easy outs by the fielding team. This describes how the hitter is being '*punished*'. Even though the hitter has aligned their bat to the ball much better in Type 2 than in Type 3 or 4, they are punished by being 'out' instead of just having a strike against them.

The most important thing here is to not get tied up in the details of the specific measurements. Whether the types of misalignment are extremely precise is not the point. The point is that even though the hitter has put their bat much closer to the desired point of impact in Type 2 misalignment than in Type 3 or 4, they get a much less desirable outcome. Again, hitters are punished for being closer to their goal than when they miss altogether.

Axiom #5—Break the Cycle

If we really are going to improve hitting, we can't just sit back and expect it to happen by itself. Action is required to achieve the objective—there is no learning by osmosis, and there are no serendipitous awakenings.

Skepticism is reasonable. But both doubt and skepticism can be addressed with knowledge, logic and reason. And if you continue to doubt, but are intrigued, I invite you to take a risk and just keep reading.

Our belief must be that something must change. If you have any doubt, rely on Einstein's definition of insanity. If we think we can get dramatic improvement without any change, he said we are 'insane'.

I have a good friend (Chris) who takes joy in being a contrarian—a true devil's advocate. Chris argues opposing opinions as a way of checking one's data regarding outlandish claims such as, "I've invented a new way to swing the baseball bat."

If ever I fail his devil's advocate tests he dismisses my argument as 'drinking the Kool-Aid'. To be true to the lessons my friend has taught me, we will throughout the book check and re-check the steps to ensure they are reasonable and logical. However, once we have done so, we must move to take action.

Always Build on a Strong Foundation

The foundation of these Axioms lay at the heart of the Pivotal Swing®. We will build upon these 5 Axioms using the methodology I have confirmed will improve any process I have been involved with and countless others I have read about. Dr. Kiemele and Air Academy Associates have written books about and trained thousands of Fortune 500 company members to use these methods successfully to improve unimaginable types and quantities of processes. Let's be clear, if you think either the general or specific objectives of this book are impossible, you should probably stop reading. From this point forward we are not only operating on the belief that they are possible, but also that we will show what changes will get us there, why those changes are important and how to execute or implement them. I am excited about leading you on this journey and the opportunity to show you how to do something you probably didn't think possible.

Accuracy and Precision

It is self-evident that in order to improve hitting; we have to do something different than what has been done since the time of Ted Williams. But we had .400 hitters in the past with the 'old' method of swinging so isn't the problem simply that pitchers have gotten better? Exactly. Pitchers have gotten better while batters have stayed basically the same. Whereas most pitchers only excel in two or three pitches, there are over a dozen commonly used pitching techniques. That increased ability to keep the batter guessing has served as a strong advantage for pitchers—and the common view is that batters really only have the one choice: to swing, or not to swing.

And here is a moment of revelation. In order to see a significant improvement in hitting we need to improve the accuracy and precision of the hitter's bat placement. Wow! Profound, isn't it? My brother's comment to me would be, 'You have a keen sense for the obvious." We are going to improve the accuracy of a process that must be executed in 0.2 seconds. Though to some it may seem obvious, the achievement is anything but.

A swing, with strategic changes, generates enormous improvements in the end by making small modifications early in the process. To achieve this aim we must break down the swing into its most basic elements and diligently assess every key step, holding on to what works, and dropping what doesn't. What remains, a purified, distilled swing more precisely and reliably aligns the bat with the exact same plane as the ball and results in improved accuracy. What happens when we then add more productive elements to the purified swing is nothing less than an improved hitting process.

Hardest Thing to Do in Sports?

I don't think there is much controversy over this anymore. It was debated for quite a while. However, the world seems to have adopted what Hall of Famer Ted Williams said, "The hardest thing to do in sports is hit a baseball," especially when facing a MLB pitcher.

Take a Google of the phrase—"Hardest thing to do in sports", and you'll get over 3 million hits. In the top 50 places over 90% listed 'hitting a baseball in major league baseball as the hardest. If one Googles—"hitting a baseball hardest thing to do," there are about 13 million hits. Although the question will always be up for debate, I'm satisfied, but not just because of a couple Google searches. Isn't it possible all those Google hits were written by people who were just drinking the Kool-Aid?

Is It Really That Hard?

OK, let's get into a few more points about the general complexity of the hitting process. Let's break it down a little.

For starters, the thing were trying to hit is moving, and it's moving damn fast. Although some pitchers consistently throw in excess of 100 MPH, that's not really the norm. But a measly 90 MPH really is pretty standard. And at 90 MPH a pitch will travel the 60 feet 6 inches (18.44 m.) to home plate in about 0.4 seconds—the time it takes for a hummingbird to flap its wings 5 times.

Now consider the hitter's location, just a couple feet from the pitcher's target. Good luck staring that deadly weapon down without a flinch, yet alone with a sense of composure and accuracy. Protective devices from ear-flaps on helmets and arm/leg guards for batters, to shin guards and throat shields to protect the catcher and umpire, and yet severe injuries continue to occur. Yes, that ball moving that fast is a deadly weapon.

Few of us have stared down a major league pitcher from behind home plate. Those who have know all too well that ball does not travel in a straight line! It moves sideways or curves. And sometimes, it moves a lot!

A pitched baseball only takes 0.4 seconds to reach home plate. It takes at least half that time for the hitter to decide if the pitch is good enough to swing at, leaving only 0.2 seconds to actually execute the swing. Ooops, we just lost half of that very little time we allotted the hitter.

So standing just feet from the target, with a ball travelling at 90 miles per hour, the batter with full composure, must generate 70 MPH of bat speed—accurately. The average speed at the head of a golf club is 100 miles per hour, with golfers like Tiger Woods swinging in excess of 125 miles per hour. But the higher club-head speeds are generated by a bigger arc, and a much lighter material. The baseball bat is shorter, heavier and takes much more brute force to maneuver than a golf club, though with similarly compact margins of error, as shown by the fractions of an inch that separate a line-drive from a pop fly.

The biggest difference between the golf swing and the baseball swing is that the golf ball is *not moving!* The difference between hitting a stationary golf ball and a pitched baseball moving at 90 MPH is HUGE! And to be clear; I have also played a fair amount of golf.

I know that hitting a golf ball is not easy—at least for me, but it's a walk in the park compared to swinging a 32 ounce wooden bat, 70 miles per hour, and connecting it with the 'sweet spot' (+/- 3/8 of an inch from the center-line) of a ball travelling and 90 miles per hour, spinning and moving sideways.

Small Change Can Produce Big Improvements!!

Sometimes a small change can produce a big improvement. But it is also true that a small change can produce a big problem. This may be even easier to relate to in our personal lives. Car accidents are very often the cause of a small change—a faulty break light, a good song on the radio, or a drunk driver weaving in traffic can all result in a big problem.

In the context of process improvement this concept is paramount. When looking to improve a process, the data will often lead to a small change that results in low-cost, high-profit improvements.

With the hitting process, we earlier mentioned that typically there is only 0.2 seconds available to execute a swing. If we are able to make a small change in the swing process to reduce its time of execution by 0.04 seconds, we produce a 20% gain in the time a hitter has to watch the pitch and decide whether to swing or not. 20 percent more time anyone?

Any batter knows the importance of accurate bat placement yet little or nothing has been done to strategically improve it. We have already discussed it twice, and in future Innings we will do so again. However, at that time, we will do so in the context of small changes that make big improvements. If we are strategic in our decisions, we will uncover at least one small change resulting in significant improvements over the current art and science of hitting. By identifying a core level process improvement—even if it is considered a small change, we will dramatically improve hitting.

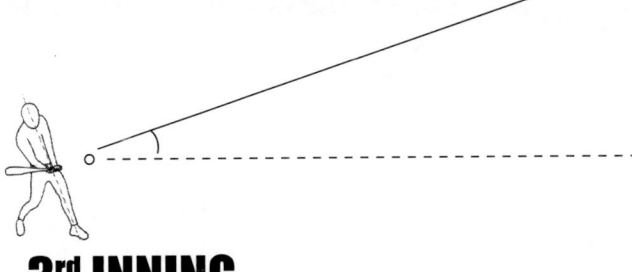

3rd INNING
What is Process Improvement All About?

Because of my experience as an engineer, manager and director involving process improvement (PI), I view the game of baseball from a different perspective than the baseball establishment. And although I love the game, I am excited to challenge some of its traditions (though beer and hotdogs I'll leave just the way they are). The Six Sigma tools, and other similar methods of organizing and interpreting data, give a whole new way to view the hitting process. Although the tools are not new to many in business, they are new to the world of baseball, and were perhaps most successfully exemplified in 2002 by the Oakland A's general manager Billy Beane, who as told in the book, Moneyball, used statistics in the selection of players.

Player selection is a business process. Beane and his advisors used statistics to decide which players to have on the team and when to play them in certain game scenarios. Whether he or any of them had been exposed to Six Sigma or PI was not revealed. There is a huge difference in applying statistics to member selection than applying PI tools to improve individual player performance. Here is an analogy. Beane's method is more like deciding the ingredients in the formula for Coca-Cola. The objective of this book is more like improving the method to make a ka-zillion bottles of Coca-Cola, all exactly the same, maintain all the health regulations for food production, maintain all the company and government regulations for safety in manufacturing, maintain all the government regulations for environmental impact, maintain all the accounting regulations of Sarbanes-Oxley Act, maintain all the IRS regulations *and* distribute them all over the world on a daily basis. Though only an analogy, that my friends is why I warned you that this is not going to be a casual read. It is also why I view this book as the *equivalent of 'Moneyball' on steroids*.

Part of the challenge here is to introduce the concept of process improvement (PI) without losing touch with the heart of the game of baseball. Though PI is founded on scientific methods, we don't need to be scientists to apply it, and though we may stray a bit into technical discussion, for my sake, as much as yours, I'll try to refrain from too much jargon. I too am no rocket scientist and much happier when experts speak in simple, logical terms.

My Mentor

Much of my corporate experience has been with Sony Electronics, and in the early years, primarily focused on manufacturing process improvement and quality systems. In various roles in Sony, I constantly sought out new ways to improve our processes, whether relating to a manufacturing process, or a better way to organize the staff and functions. I was eventually promoted to Sony's Director of Six Sigma Deployment, where I organized the training of our management, engineers and staff on how to make processes more effective.

I met one of my mentors, Keito Nakazawa, Vice-President of Engineering and Quality, at Sony's San Diego facility. I had always viewed myself as a business engineer at heart, more than specialized in electronics & electrical engineering. Our similarities led us down a path of applying business engineering principles, in which we so believed, to the manufacturing and quality systems.

From the day I met him I was intrigued by the ease with which he saw through incredibly complicated decisions and distilled simple, effective solutions. I asked him once, what was the secret to this skill?

"I let the data make the decision," he replied. At Sony we had hundreds of people involved with hundreds of processes, and Nakazawa convinced me that by gathering the right data, any decision, no matter how many people were involved, becomes easier. And yet he also went a step further and argued that by gathering the right data, almost anyone can make the right decision in any context, because with the right information, the proper course is made self-evident.

As the years have worn on his words have grown into a mantra, let the data make the decision, let the data make the decision, let the data make the decision.

Process Improvement vs. Six Sigma

Before implementing Six Sigma at Sony we had to answer one big question. Could all our process improvement efforts really be effectively consolidated under just one platform? There were no doubts about so doing in manufacturing operations; however the complexity lied in whether we could fully engage the non-manufacturing operations (accounting, accounts payable, purchasing, marketing, sales, HR or even legal) into pursuit of such a lofty goal. Our conclusion though not simple was: yes, it could.

Since reaching that conclusion was not simple, and further complicating our task, there are actually several different methods of deploying Six Sigma. One method is based on the methods employed by Motorola, the birthplace of Six Sigma, and focused more on the scientific which is more difficult to deploy on a massive scale. Whereas the other method, deployed by Allied Signal and GE, is considered more practical, and easier to apply to staff with a wider range of functions and experience.

The corporate process improvement leadership at Sony (Japan) had already assessed deployment of Motorola's version of Six Sigma and rejected it as not being the right fit for our company. Motorola's version had migrated to Japan by that time; however they were unaware that GE and Allied signal had developed an alternative deployment style with more emphasis on practical and company-wide application. My colleagues and I on the other hand had learned of the 2nd method and managed to convince the corporate leadership in Japan to invest $10 million to deploy this set of Process Improvement tools on a global scale.

A key aspect in improving a process is getting those closest to it trained to use the tools. Although some were trained to high levels, many were trained at a more practical application level. With their practical training they were able to start breaking larger processes down into smaller ones. Mapping a process leads to clear visualization of the overall process, including flaws, duplications, inadequacies and potential improvements. When the trainees first dissected Sony's processes, inefficiencies naturally rose to the surface and solutions were revealed. In other cases the trainees formed project teams often seeking the knowledge of higher level trained members to aid in determining which data would best inform their decisions, gathered the data, formulated possible improvements, and tested the changes to determine which changes led to most effective improvements.

Let the data make the decision.

We found that implementation needed to come from the top. If the leaders of an organization aren't convinced they will benefit by training people and allowing them to address process improvement, it is almost impossible to effect improvements in the processes of those organizations. Such change requires great will, and on the corporate level that will-power must come from above. However, if a leader isn't open to change, isn't initiating the proper training and encouraging the staff to ask the right questions or gather the right data, the organization will almost always stumble and fall.

There is a general tendency for many of us to resist change. Not always. Some folks are more open to change in general. As usual, those most comfortable with breaking from tradition are those who have experienced failures of the status quo and come to believe that the new process is worth the investment necessary to deploy. Is every change perfect? Of course not! Did the staff learn to be more effective at gathering the right data and selecting the best improvements? Yes.

And as they improved, they gathered and discovered more and better tools that allowed them to see more deeply and accurately into the processes. Until little by little, we all became a bit more like Nakazawa, able to gather the right data and 'let the data make the decision'. The right data often allowed them to see through the clutter at simple, low-cost solutions.

Gaining Acceptance of Process Improvement

Without both understanding of the problem and acceptance of the solution, implementing the improvements we develop, in any field, is much more complicated. So the first step to accepting that process improvement can improve a hitter's success is to understand that many of the planets most successful companies have applied PI tools to improve a wide and diverse range of processes.

As with most large companies, Sony had the least resistance with implementation in the manufacturing groups. Most manufacturing groups have some form or PI already in place and the Six Sigma deployment helped organize and create common knowledge between these groups. It was harder to get groups like accounting, sales and legal to look at their processes. This kind of data and analysis was new to them.

As Sony continued to deploy PI, more organizations joined the effort. When those organizations saw our initial success first hand they became willing to try the techniques in their group.

By breaking down this resistance to change our company executives saw massive benefits, and like the old maxim goes, success breeds success, as was readily apparent in our large scale corporate deployment. But just like in sports, not every trainee nor every organization within Sony was successful to the same degree.

Though not directly competing against another company, at least in this context, other forms of beneficial competition did eventual take hold. Competition like which team completes a task most efficiently or saves the most money or creates the best product led to a more effective Sony on every level.

One of the primary reasons Sony, Motorola, GE & others were so vehement about the pursuit of process improvement was the disparity in processes across divisions and corporate structures. While in a manufacturing process, lower than a 98% yield brought lots of attention, other processes in the same company are as low as 30% and nobody was raising Cain. The latter depicts a group that isn't asking the right questions or assessing their processes effectively. Now, in baseball, batting .300 is actually pretty impressive, but every mistake in Sony or any company costs money, and closing those gaps saved us a lot of wasted resources and money.

In one particularly interesting instance we learned that one of our accounts payable operations automated bill paying system was only successful thirty-three percent of the time. Yes, for every three invoices we received, only one was automatically paid through the computers. That meant that 2 out of 3 had some discrepancy in the purchase order, receiving, accepting, invoice entry or handling of the payment process. This required people to investigate and fix the discrepancies. Once some members were trained they measured and found this condition. 'Letting the data make the decision' in this case led to a clear decision this performance was totally unacceptable. Once they started a disciplined approach to assessing all the sub-processes involved, they improved rapidly. They found what eventually all find: the methods work on all kinds of processes.

While at Sony I focused on just one segment of the company, Sony Electronics, though Corporate was actively working to implement the tools in operations around the world. We eventually developed a method for gathering data on the deployment, such as number of people trained, number of projects open, number of projects completed and the amount of savings earned.

As already mentioned, over the first three years of Sony's Six Sigma deployment we saved nearly a half billion dollars. On one hand corporate leadership was thrilled to achieve such good results. Who of us wouldn't love to save hundreds of millions of dollars? On the other hand, someone had to answer why we were losing hundreds of millions of dollars in the first place. And the answer to that question can sometimes be embarrassing. The key is to keep improving and do better than your competition.

In effective deployment an organization should work to improve processes directly focused on both top line (revenue) growth and bottom line (cost) reduction. And using Sigma Six, Sony was doing both.

The uncomfortable situation baseball's establishment will soon have to answer, is why it is acceptable for batters to only succeed 30 percent of the time. Are they asking the right questions, measuring the right things or gathering the right data? If they were, like we will show, 'let the data make the decision'.

The Method

There are many PI tools. Not all are required to evaluate every process. The tools range from somewhat simple and intuitive to very complex, scientific and mathematical. Determining which tool is necessary where, is an essential element of process improvement. Yes, it was just as Nakazawa had told me many years before. By choosing the correct data to gather, the solution to fixing most problems usually rises to the surface. We are extra lucky when changes are not only clear but also relatively simple.

An unevaluated process in place for years is ripe with opportunities to make simple changes that will often yield wide-ranging improvements. The first step is to gather data on the performance characteristics of the process to be improved.

Most companies already gather data on at least some of their processes. Is that sufficient? Does that mean their processes are maximizing efficiency? Unfortunately, not all data is created equal, and *what* is measured is just as important as taking measurements. In fact, it is quite common that inaccurate or wrong data misleads management. And so, building on my mentor's mantra, I began to question whether or not the decrease in baseball hitting averages is an example of management gathering the wrong data. Maybe they have allowed the status quo that pitching has improved and hitting hasn't to be their mantra. That will only change when the mold is broken by a better hitting process. That ups the ante and a new competition begins.

As a fan of baseball it was easy for me, drawing on a lifetime of observations to accept the desire to improve hitting as a core value of both baseball hitters and coaches. I expect that all of them—from the worst hitter in the majors to the best the league has to offer—are interested in finding room for improvement. Has management not asked the right questions? Maybe they just didn't realize that process improvement tools can work for them. We will review this later when we ask the question—is baseball a game or a business? Regardless of which is the case, or if it's all of the above, what is necessary to return to an era of .400 hitters is nothing less than a minor revolution—and I imagine the powers that be are comfortable with the status quo and will resist embracing a significantly new way of swinging the bat.

Additional Depth on Process Improvement

After 23 years of working with various members refining processes at Sony—ranging from manufacturing issues to computer display design processes—the process improvement strategy and methods have time and again proven themselves viable, and every time I see it succeed it fills me with a greater sense of confidence. Time and again my colleagues and I have seen PI tools used on hundreds of processes and consistently they have proven themselves beneficial when the right questions are asked and right data is gathered. Just like Nakazawa said all those years ago, the right data itself, when interpreted using the right tools almost seems to make its own decision, telling us, this is what you do. This is the solution to your problem. This is the most efficient way. And I believe, as do those who have seen the swing in action, that once the protectors of the baseball status quo are presented with the data we have gathered, they too will come to the same conclusion. The Pivotal Swing® will change baseball.

As with many projects in Sony it became clear that some relatively small changes could generate major improvements—though small is a relative term. By small I mean that many aspects of the current hitting process do not need to be changed. By small, I also mean that most hitters can make the changes in a very short period of time. And after appropriately analyzing the data it is not hard to see just what those small changes are. In fact, it turns out the changes are not radical in the least.

Before going on, I want to clarify a key aspect of PI. Essentially, all implementers of PI tools seek core level process improvements—improvements to the most fundamental nature of a process that leads to repeatable gains in the desired outputs. Anyone who uses the new process will achieve better results than they got using the old process. Understandably there are different levels of improvement gains to any process change. Large gains are always desirable, though not always possible. The key is that when a core level process improvement is achieved all those who implement the change will achieve improved results. Think back to the Fosbury Flop. Since the introduction of that method no one has returned to the old method of high jumping. For those seeking to improve a process, finding such a core level improvement is like hitting a line-drive in baseball. As soon as the bat hits the ball, you know it's a winner!

But we are not interested in change for the sake of change, and we will not be haphazard in our method. Disciplined application of PI tools requires that we focus on how newly developed changes affect the outputs or results of a process. Just like some changes lead to desirable, increased outputs, other changes can be destructive. Our objective is to find the right changes that improve the good results and minimize the bad results. Even better is if the change altogether eliminates the most undesired outputs. In this way we can say our proposed changes are focused on the outputs.

Superstition as a Form of Resistance to Change

There are different degrees of superstition. A lucky hat inherited from dad, a stinky pair of socks, or a ratty beard might all become as essential to a player's game as their grip on the bat, or the pocket of their glove—and asking a player to give up that hat or those socks or that beard may be as difficult as asking them to change the way they hold their bat. But the Pivotal Swing® must overcome such superstitions. The logic and details of the data will convert even the most adamant resistors to change.

Superstitions, like all habits, are hard to change, but in the end, when a good habit is formed it remains indelibly imprinted in the mind as does a bad habit, as will be the case with the Pivotal Swing®. It is important to remember that any process can be improved. Any new processes that work in baseball will eventually supersede any existing process within the game, including a new way to swing the bat. I say this mostly because although the new process will deliver far better results, it too will someday become outdated, and we must not let superstition take hold even in the case of a scientifically derived technique such as the Pivotal Swing®. Even at the end of this book we are not done. The improvements that we have found are not the only improvements that can be made. They are just the improvements developed and introduced so far—and once the new technique is mastered we will continue the development of the next level improvements.

All process improvements occur in stages. When too much variation exists in a process, the more sophisticated tools lose their edge or effectiveness.

Therefore larger variations should be reduced or eliminated by the simplest tools possible first. We can always come back later and apply more sophisticated tools when the situation is right. That situation is when the simpler (less sophisticate tools) can no longer find improvements. I can clearly see where we can use some additional tools to improve the hitting process further. And when that time comes it will be exciting indeed, though that time is in the future.

A More Sinister Side of Change

And yet, the better mousetrap doesn't always make it to market. Likely, improved products and processes come at the detriment of existing brands. And those who teach the old technique and own the old brands, the guardians of the status quo, won't likely just stand by as they become outdated. Instead they will either join the revolution or be in opposition by taking whatever steps they can to ensure the new process never sees the light of day

The existing pro coaches may lose the most. They are the ones that 'should' have developed this and will likely be the ones to push back the most. I will remain optimistic that they will see the logic and want to lead the movement into the new era of .400 hitters. Though in the end, as with all core level process improvements, the real loser is anyone who doesn't implement the changes.

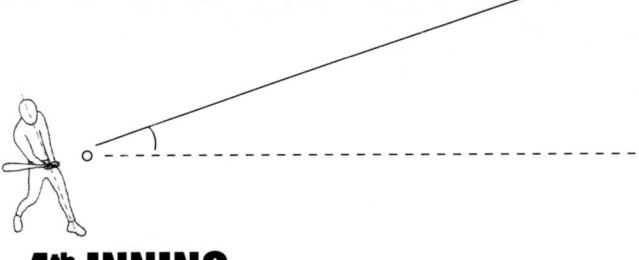

4th INNING
Is Hitting an Art or a Science?

Though there are proponents of both views, this may remain a conundrum. If hitting were just a science PI tools most likely would have already been applied by someone else. If it were just an art there would be little use in coaching at all, and those with born talent would succeed while the rest languished. That hitting is teachable, makes it a science, though that it escapes ever being fully understood makes it an art too.

As we have already discussed, the half art, half science swing is in the end nothing more than a process (Axiom #2). It is as much like building a car as it is like painting a fresco. Yet both of these represent aspects of both art and science too. And just like in science, there are processes for creating art. Painters don't just sit down and paint a masterpiece. They plan, organize, study anatomy, practice figure drawings, and goof up a whole bunch before the masterpiece is ever actually realized.

In 'The Science of Hitting' by Ted Williams and coauthor John Underwood, Williams writes, "Everybody knows how to hit but very few really do." And in response to complaints common by players during the 1970's that "the ball is dead," the coauthors argued, "The ball isn't dead, the hitters are, from the neck up." These authors understood that a successful hitter is a master of his or her mind.

In contrast, in Tony Gwynn and Roger Vaughan's book 'The Art of Hitting' the authors argue "The good hitters develop an understanding of why they do what they do …. Knowing yourself isn't your coach's responsibility; it's your responsibility …. No, hitting isn't a science. It's an art. That's why it's so satisfying, and so much fun." And yet, Williams' book explores both the art and the science of hitting, as does Gwynn's, which even includes a Foreword written by Williams himself. So with the two greatest hitters of their generations both opposed to one another in the titles of their books, and yet somehow also in perfect harmony, the distinction between the art and science of hitting really is lost.

And although I clearly fall more in alignment with Williams' book title and a more scientific approach to hitting, as a die-hard Padres fan Tony Gwynn is one of my favorite hitters of all time. In his book he promotes the 'art' yet in practice he is one of the most scientific. Acknowledging the importance the "gut" plays in hitting—that there is a sense which cannot ever be fully taught—the focus of the remainder of this book is on how one uses PI tools in a scientific, yet practical way to find and implement the changes that are best for achieving our desired objective of creating the first .400 hitter in nearly 70 years.

I will venture to say that the folks who truly believe that hitting is just an art will be more inclined to accept the status quo—they won't choose to look for tools or methods that might help them or someone else break down the hitting process into its pieces and find room for improvements to the steps of hitting that will improve the overall process.

On the other hand, those who believe there is a way to successfully analyze and develop processes to improve baseball will find in me a kindred spirit. For these people will undoubtedly be critical of my assessment of the hitting process, and double-check it along the way. In some cases they may even conclude there are better ways to create a .400 hitter. And let me be the first to say, I don't believe the findings and methods in this book are the final answer, and I'm anxious to see what other methods the application of process improvement to hitting will generate. Even the Pivotal Swing® itself is a work in progress, which I plan to continue to develop. I expect I will be joined by players and coaches that are willing to lead this change, and maybe by some well equipped fans as well.

From experience I am confident that any process can be improved. It isn't necessarily easy. But I am confident the game and the swing will continue to develop. After we achieve .400, maybe .450 or .500 will be the new target. Baseball will continue to be loved the world over, and with every new draft, and every new coach it will continue to change ever so slightly, though it will be rare to have such a chance as we now have to be a part of a revolution in the game.

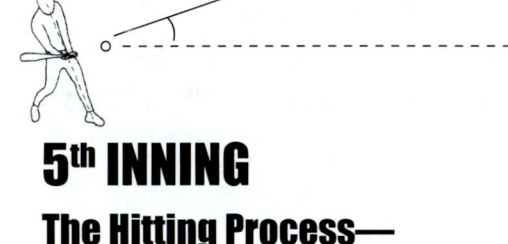

5th INNING
The Hitting Process—
Inputs & Outputs

But between now and the revolution stands a fair amount of data collection and assessment, and like any core level Process Improvement (PI), this will require some patience.

One of the beginning PI tools is to identify the Inputs and Outputs of the process being analyzed. If a change to our process strengthens one productive output and yet also strengthens a destructive output, the end result is neutral. Therefore, we must be mindful of the impact a change to part of the process might have on other apparently unrelated parts of the process, especially its Outputs. An improvement to the process that results in both strengthening a productive Output *and* eliminates a detrimental Output is not only beneficial but sought after.

Businesses and life are a conglomeration of processes. A common occurrence in the relationship between processes is that the Output of one process becomes the Input of another process. It mainly occurs when the processes are sequential. The Output of the 'build a car' process is the car. The car then becomes the Input to 'let's drive to the game' process. In this case the car is both an Output and Input. This explanation is not rhetorical. It is preparing you for the actual situation with the hitting process.

An example of sequential processes in baseball would be: the outputs of the hitter's set-up or preparation process become the inputs to the swing process. How the hitter selects where they will be in the batter's box is not trivial. It is common to see various forms of measurements, such as extending the bat to a target location on home plate, used by the hitter to ensure they are in the same spot they have selected for hundreds of swings in batting practice. Though set-up is completely separate from the swing process, they are both part of the hitting process and success is dependent upon both being executed precisely as practiced.

When we describe a process as 'robust' what we mean is a process that is less affected by operating conditions such as the batter's strength, pitch speed, or weather. Robust is good. It is a form of an output but it is based upon the design of the process not the execution of the hitter. If changes are made that increase the robustness of a process, they typically result in some form of positive output measurement. If a new hitting process has better balance when delivered an off-speed pitch that is a more robust process, and will be demonstrable in improved statistics and metrics. In this example the metrics that might improve are getting more hits or fewer strike-outs, or both. A more robust process is highly desired.

Other examples of operating conditions are the shape of a baseball field, ambient temperature, wind, lighting (sun, night lights, intensity, angle, source, etc.), the ball weight, color, and shape of the background behind the pitcher, quality (shape) of the ground in the batter's box, etc. We consider them but not at the same level as Inputs and Outputs because the hitter has no control over them. As mentioned above, a more robust process is one that produces better Outputs regardless of the operating conditions.

Let's look at the first primary element of this PI tool: Inputs. Inputs can include things that the hitter does or doesn't have control over. We will list some; listing all of them would get too cumbersome. These will allow you to conceptualize Inputs that are being considered:

1. Watch/see the ball
2. Physical strength, tone and quickness
3. Location relative to the plate
4. Size & shape of the bat (some choice within regulations)
5. Steady head position (head movement)
6. Balance
7. Confidence (obviously mental rather than physical aspect)
8. Fear
9. Pitcher and the pitch

The best example of an Input that the hitter doesn't have control over is the pitcher. All the elements of what the pitcher does to deliver the pitch are inputs to the hitting process. Pitchers have significant differences in how they deliver the pitch. Some 'hide' the ball longer than others and that makes it harder for the hitter to assess whether to swing at that pitch. Pitches also come in a wide variety of speeds. Note that there is not only variation from pitcher to pitcher in the speed, but also in the choice of pitch from the same pitcher. A key weapon in the arsenal of pitchers is to use a change in speed to cause the hitter to be off balance.

Getting back to robustness for a moment, we can add clarity. A more robust process will give better results with variations of the Inputs as well as the operating conditions. Since the variation in pitchers and their choice of pitches is wide indeed, a more robust process delivers better results regardless of those variations in comparison to a less robust process. When we add the variations of all the Inputs and combine them with all the uncontrollable operating conditions, it is logical that a more robust process is what we are pursuing.

Not All Inputs are Physical/Mechanical

The list of Inputs above includes: Fear and Confidence. Those are mental issues and have nothing to do with physical strength or the mechanics of the bat, ball or field. Without prior experience in this area, it would be uncommon for most of you to realize some of these Inputs. Consideration of them is even less likely. That is why we use these PI tools. They help us to look closely at a process and see it more clearly than we have before or without the use of a tool.

Fear can have a huge impact on the ability of a hitter to produce great outputs. Fear doesn't have to be real, only imagined. Whether real or imagined, either way it will impact Outputs. Fear of a 90 MPH pitched baseball would be 'real' if the pitcher were to tell the hitter I am going to hit you with it. A more likely scenario is that hitters have a mental image of being hit and the ensuing injury or pain it will cause. Standing in the batter's box will test the hitter's ability to deal with the Fear (real or imagined). We have all seen the Little Leaguer, cowering in the back of the batter's box with debilitating Fear. That Fear is sufficient to prevent that player from using any of their knowledge or skills of hitting. Dramatically more subtle is the Fear residing in a MLB player. Only a small amount can impact a process that has to be executed in 0.2 seconds. Though it is well known that very few pitches hit a batter, the hitter is tested on every pitch as to whether they can control the Fear to eliminate any debilitating impact on the execution of their hitting process.

Can an Input also be an Output?

There are two very unique Inputs: Balance and Confidence. They are unique because they are both an Input and Output. The earlier exercise on this topic now fits into place. A further exemplification of the uniqueness is how the Input Balance affects the hitting process and the Output Balance. The simple description is that if the hitter is out of balance at the start of the swing, success is doomed and the hitter will most likely still be out of Balance at the end of the swing. Similarly, if the hitting process causes the hitter to lose their Balance, success will also be doomed. When the Outputs are analyzed later in this Inning, we will address Balance as an Output, for now we will view it as an Input.

Confidence though also mental is known by most to have a significant impact on ones performance.

Parents know this and constantly shout encouragement to their child in order to enhance their Confidence. These efforts are not only for young players. MLB coaches and players are constantly trying to bolster the Confidence of their teammates. It is not uncommon to see some pretty radical fans that are getting their 2 cents in on the subject as well.

Confidence and its impact on both players and teams is a highly publicized subject. Some claim it to be the most important Input. Motivational writers and gurus are promulgators of such views. Some even believe that the performance of a player can be improved by increasing their level of Confidence without an increase in knowledge or improvement in their process. I'm not interested in arguing that point. I'll always place my bet on increased knowledge and a more robust process winning that contest. Suffice it to say: Confidence is very important and improving it by practice and increased knowledge can improve a player's performance. Other than trying to write an entire book on this subject, I think we can all agree that the Input of Confidence has a definitive impact on the hitter's Outputs (performance). Whether it is the most important Input will have to remain on the battlefield of controversy. We will focus on improving the knowledge and process and let someone else fight that battle.

A couple issues I have against claiming it is the 'most' important Input are control and measurability. Fear, Confidence or any mental factor is very hard to measure. As you will see, measuring is very important in the application of PI tools. If we can't measure it; we can't quantify it properly. A key aspect of using PI tools is that we vary the inputs in conjunction with process improvements and then measure the change in the outputs. To assess the effectiveness of an improvement to the process we need to measure two (2) important things. First, did the Outputs get better as a result of the process change? Second, did the Outputs get better with more or less of each Input? The second question is assessing the robustness of the process. With lack of measurability in Confidence or any mental factor, it's more difficult to effectively assess the results. Use of the PI tool is significantly hindered.

Sometimes we have to work harder at determining the best way to measure items. If we don't have a way, we may have to find a way. Many years ago we didn't know the speed of pitches. With the aid of some smart people developing the radar gun, it is now relatively easy to measure the speed of pitches.

The radar gun gives us a quantitative measurement. If we can't get a quantitative measurement, we may have to rely on a qualitative measure. Though I don't have a quantitative measurement of Confidence, we can do so qualitatively. It was easy to qualitatively assess the Little Leaguer cowering in the back of the batter's box had very low Confidence. Similarly, the quintessential high Confidence example is when 'The Babe' pointed his bat, in the 5th game of the 1932 World Series, to centerfield and proceeded to hit the next pitch over the centerfield fence. We will always use quantitative measures when they are available and only resort to qualitative measures when they are not.

Assessing Process Robustness

In connection with assessing robustness of a process, we need to vary the Inputs and measure the changes in the Outputs. To determine if a specific process improvement is beneficial, we would measure the process Outputs before the change and then again after the change. If the change improves the process

Outputs over a wider range of Inputs, we then classify the improved process as more robust.

Along with only having qualitative measures of Confidence or Fear, we also don't have a precise method of control. We have ways to vary some of the Inputs like location to home plate, size of the bat and speed of pitches. Measuring the changes in the Outputs in those cases are possible. Ernie Banks reduced the weight of his bat (an Input) by 3 oz. in 1955 and hit 44 home-runs. In 1954 he hit 19 home-runs. A quantitative change of an Input resulted in a quantitative change on a positive Output, both measurable. By letting the data make the decision, it is easy for anyone to conclude that he continued to use the 3 oz. lighter bat.

Assessing robustness of a process change for Inputs like 'Watch the ball', Confidence or Fear must resort to qualitative measures. In addition to the qualitative comments earlier on Confidence, as a coach I could often assess that a young player was not 'Watching the ball' when he pulled his head. Though not measurable, qualitatively it was easy for me to see that when his swing missed the ball, it was due to the control of his head (an Input) not the swing process, causing the measurably detrimental Output. Along with difficulties in measuring are difficulties in controlling Inputs like Confidence. Assessing if a particular process improvement is more robust must then rely on qualitative judgment. With the right level of understanding about measuring both qualitatively and quantitatively, we can move through the mire of determining which process improvements are beneficial to Outputs and robustness.

The impetus of hitting rallies remains a conundrum. Confidence must be a significant factor. Its unique property of being both and Input and Output reveals added perspective. Not only can an Input of a hitter also be an Output of that hitter, the Output of one hitter can be the Input of another hitter. This sequential aspect of processes provides insight to solving the conundrum. The Confidence (Output) of a player that just hit a line-drive off a dominating pitcher, provides Confidence (Input) to the next hitter that the pitcher is not invincible. The message is clear: I just ripped one and you can too. This adds to our understanding of why rallies build momentum. If two previous hitters provide Confidence (their Output), though measured qualitatively as two doses, to the third hitter going to bat, it would logically contribute even more Confidence (Input) to that next hitter. The motivational gurus tell us 'success breeds success'. Their message that a positive output of one endeavor (process) will be a beneficial increase to the input of another is synonymous with a 'hitting rally'. We will add even more perspective when we cover the Outputs later.

Although we can only measure Confidence qualitatively as an Input or Output, we need to understand its impact on the hitting process. My data tells me that more Confidence (Input) contributes to more Confidence (Output). More difficult is the understanding and assessment of how the hitting process changes affect Confidence (Output) of that player as well as the team. You will see what our data shows in the 8th Inning when we cover the testing.

Now Let's Look at the Outputs

It was stated earlier that Confidence and Balance are hitting process Outputs. Here is a larger list for you to assess. These are not all of the outputs but they will give us a basis for discussion and assessment.

1. Accuracy of bat-to-ball placement
2. Timing—meet the ball at the right time

3. Confidence
4. Balance
5. Energy Transfer–linked to power in the swing
6. Amount of time to execute the process
7. Were all elements of the swing process followed?
8. Performance metrics like: hits, line-drives, fair vs. foul, etc.

Appropriate comments about some details of each Output will get us rolling. They are listed in order with some consideration of their importance. 'Some' is used here because the ranking is not 'absolute'. Although we view Accuracy as most important, it is hard to say that it is absolutely more important than Timing or Confidence. However, we are quite sure that Accuracy and Timing are more important than Balance. Case in point: we have all seen a hitter fooled by a pitch and vey unbalanced, yet they manage to accurately place the bat and get a hit. In this example the hitter has produced good Accuracy and Timing but not Balance. Based on this we give Accuracy and

Timing a little higher rank. None of them can be disregarded. They are all important. The relative importance comes into consideration when we are developing improvements.

Accuracy is the Most Important Output

Accuracy of bat-to-ball placement is the most important Output. That may be controversial to some. Our primary reason for this ranking is due to the unique characteristic of baseball where the hitter is punished for being close (Axiom #4). It was also a major factor in concluding that process improvement (PI) tools will guide us toward improvements. If a hitter gets punished for missing by a small amount, reducing the causes of variation for that output will improve the process. This is not only logical but also why the practical tools in the PI arsenal will help.

As we work on developing simplifications and improvements to the hitting process, we are going to be very keen on those that improve Accuracy. In addition we must be extremely vigilant to ensure to not include any changes that reduce Accuracy.

Note that the Inputs or elements of a swing process do not typically affect only one of the Outputs.

They will often affect one of the Outputs more than others. In some cases they could cause one Output to be improved and another to be affected negatively. As improvements are developed and evaluated, their impact on the Outputs has to be measured and assessed. We have to be careful and not reject a possible improvement for the wrong reasons. We want to keep process changes that are beneficial to all or as many Outputs as possible. Similarly we want to disregard those that are detrimental to one or more Outputs.

We do expect, there are process changes that will affect multiple Outputs. Ones that do affect multiple Outputs in beneficial ways will be the ones we will want to incorporate into the 'new swing' or hitting process. Those types of improvements are increasing the robustness of the final process. Some changes being tested have inter-linkage with others. Due to these circumstances we need to try different combinations of proposed changes to find those linkages.

In preparation for the later Innings where we provide inputs on the possible process changes that will improve Accuracy and the other Outputs, I want to encourage you to study the list of Outputs and look back at the listed Inputs. The mere introduction of these specific elements may trigger ideas for improvements. That is one of the reasons for using PI tools, especially 'practical' ones like this. They help us see the process more effectively and precisely. Specific identity of Inputs and Outputs can lead your thoughts toward possible improvements. Commonly, these lists will change as you work on improving a process. They are now much different than when we began. As you review them, try to identify some ideas for improvements. You can compare your list to ours later.

Confidence is listed relatively high on the Output list. More important than its relative position is the mere fact that it is on the list. To be thorough we must review process change impacts on all the outputs and it will be included regardless of its position. We won't restate all the comments made earlier about Confidence as an Input, because they also apply as an Output. Along with Confidence being a 'mental' characteristic as an Input, measurement as an Output will also have to be qualitatively. 'Fear' another mental characteristic was also an Input and Output. Though it could be here on the Output list, we chose not to include it because its impact is less as an Output, and confirms that not all possible Outputs are listed. We are focusing on the key Outputs.

Energy Transfer—More Important than Bat Speed

Output #5 could be easily misunderstood. The purpose isn't to assess if the hitter is swinging as hard as they can. Power is good, but not at the expense of Accuracy, Timing or Balance. This may help make some of my earlier comments more clear. Earlier I mentioned that we have to be careful of changes (possible improvements) that help one Output and hurt one or more others. Swinging very hard can improve power. However, it can (and does) have severely negative impacts on Accuracy, Timing and Balance. Thus, it is very important to note that this Output is looking at power in the sense of energy transferred to the ball. We are not interested in bat speed alone.

Energy Transfer to the baseball has a number of factors involved.

1. Pitched ball speed

2. Bat speed—opposite direction to the pitched ball

3. Accuracy of bat-to-ball placement

4. Timing of wrist roll-over

#1 & #2 are quite obvious. #4 is a detail that hasn't been mentioned yet. The importance isn't real high at this point. It is here because when the top-hand rolls over the bottom-hand during the swing, there is an increase in speed of the tip of the bat. Although our general perspective is that most hitters will hit the ball before the roll-over occurs, if roll-over happens during or just before contact the amount of energy transfer would be higher when all other conditions are the same.

#3 like #4 may not have been in your initial thoughts. An explanation of this needs reference back to the Outputs. It is commonly understood that an Output of the hitting process is to 'hit the ball'. That could easily be #3 in this list. However, we have chosen to describe 'hit the ball' more precisely with the Outputs of Accuracy and Energy Transfer. Once in your view, I don't think it is hard to realize that the amount of energy transferred to the ball will be greatly affected by the Accuracy.

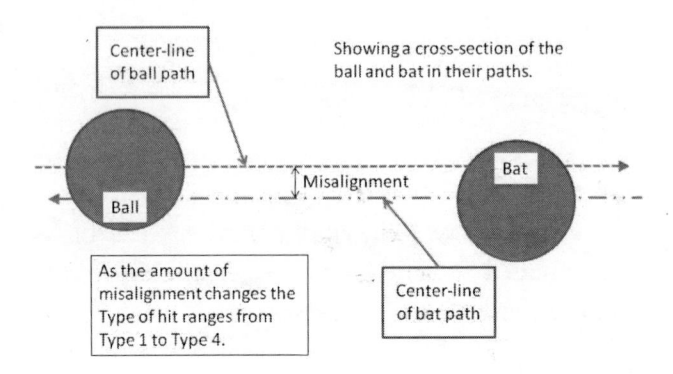

Diagram 1 shows:
- Center-line of ball path
- Showing a cross-section of the ball and bat in their paths.
- Ball
- Misalignment
- Bat
- Center-line of bat path
- As the amount of misalignment changes the Type of hit ranges from Type 1 to Type 4.

Diagram1 - Alignment: center-line of bat-to-ball

There are some very sophisticated laws of math and physics to calculate the energy transfer based upon the difference in the alignment of the center-line of the bat to that of the ball. I doubt seriously that you want to get into those equations. Let's make it easier on ourselves. Can we agree that the amount of energy transferred to the ball is drastically reduced as the misalignment of the 2 center-lines increases? If the surface of the bat and ball were flat, that change in energy transfer may be somewhat linear. However, since the ball *and* bat are both round that Energy Transfer is reduced dramatically. The rate of change is exponential due to those rounded surfaces. This is super important in understanding the impact of the hitter getting punished in baseball for being close (Axiom #4).

These comments should dramatically increase your awareness of why Accuracy was the highest rated Output. They shed new light on how important Accuracy is to determining the best hitting process. When developing possible improvements, we must look closely at those that will improve Accuracy, because of our added understanding of the impact on Energy Transfer.

We Are Not Done With Outputs!

Looking back at the list, Output #7 may seem a little odd to you. Why would we assess whether the elements of the swing process were followed? The primary reason is for good assessment. If we are going to measure the beneficial results to the Outputs of the process change being tested, we want to be sure the entire method and change were followed or done well. We would not want to 'count' the impact on the Outputs when the defined process and change were not followed. That would skew or imbalance the assessment of whether the change is good or bad. We obviously would not want to have an ineffective assessment. That could easily lead to the wrong conclusion of what changes are good or bad. Continuation of the wrong thought process would lead us to the wrong final process. When we finalize the Pivotal Swing® process, we want it to be analytically and statistically correct on its improvements to hitting.

We can't conclude without some comments on #8. It, like #7, is about assessment and measurement. Metrics are important to measure any process, including hitting. Baseball has not been remiss by not having any hitting process metrics. However, I want to go back to my mentor's input. If we are asking the right questions and have the right metrics, usually anyone can make the right decision.

Maybe team leadership and coaches are happy with the status quo and have stopped asking the question: how do we dramatically improve the hitting process? I won't be ridiculous and state or think that no players or coaches want to improve. However, they may have fallen into a common trap of not believing or seriously pursuing the possibilities. They especially couldn't ask the questions of how to use PI tools when they don't know about them or their power to help achieve the seemingly unachievable. I came out of a different 'mold'. I don't think like the baseball industry; just in case I haven't convinced you of that yet.

I believe I told you before, that it is very often an outsider that sees the possibility for process improvements that those closest to it don't see. Baseball is prolific at gathering and posting a vast number of statistics (stats) on players. There is at least one metric that they don't measure or track that I think is necessary. It is more descriptive of the process than the current stats. If they aren't measuring the right things, it is impossible for them to use those metrics for development of an improved hitting process. We have introduced that Energy Transfer might be the one of them. Another would be classifying whether the connection (bat-to-ball) is a line-drive, somewhat well hit or poorly hit. This concept is introduced in the later Innings when we cover Testing. Hits and home-runs give some indication of energy transfer, but they are weak as a metric for the effectiveness of the Energy Transfer. They are misleading because you can get a hit by accident or even by a poorly executed hitting process. I'm really going to go out on a limb here and say that I actually think most home-runs should not be classified as line-drives.

I suppose I have to explain that one. Hey, that's reasonable. We wouldn't want you to accept inputs without some critical assessment. I made that statement because to me the perfect hit is a line-drive. Yes, there are a few home-runs that could be classified as a line-drive, but they are few and far between. Some of you would not argue that a very high fly ball that is blown by the wind over the home-run fence is a miss-hit (and not a line-drive). The harder issue would be whether you agree that many home-runs are the result of a luckily-timed upward swing that didn't miss the center-line of the ball too much and got enough energy transfer to put it over the home-run fence.

The key words in that statement are 'upward swing'. We'll get into more details of the swing plane later. Let's not get into the math or physics on this one either. If the bat is not swung in the same plane as the ball, there is a significant difference in the amount of time available to make the perfect connection. Keep in mind that we are talking about hundredths, maybe even thousandths, of a second difference. That doesn't mean it can't be done. It means that it will happen much less frequently due to the reduced amount of line-drive connection time. If you have wondered why home-runs in MLB have increased and batting averages have fallen, we have just identified one of the causes. Whether it is the primary cause needs further analysis.

It might be more appropriate to say that there hasn't been the right emphasis on Energy Transfer. With more data gathered on how many line-drives were hit (regardless if it resulted in an out or base hit) is more important than the current data. I'm not saying that we don't need to track batting average. We need that for historic and comparison purposes. However, for effective hitting and assessment of whether the method being used can be improved, the player (and teams) should also be classifying and tracking whether the hitter executed their chosen process well *and* got good Energy Transfer.

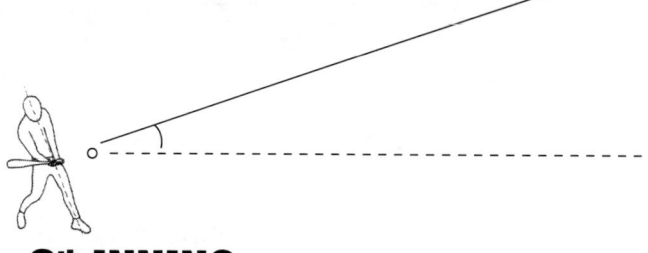

6th INNING
Getting Started on Improvements

The information given in 5th Inning should have created some ideas about possible improvements. If not, it is time to get started. Keep in mind; we will maintain the KISS principle as we proceed (Keep It Simple Statistically or a little more of a confronting version is Keep It Simple, Stupid). And though scientific, we will preferentially choose the practical tools as much as possible.

When a process improvement (PI) effort is initiated, it is standard operating procedure to look for immediate simplification. Some of the questions asked are: (1) Is there duplication? (2) What steps are insignificant to the final Outputs or are a waste of resources? (3) Which steps are possibly contributing to detrimental Outputs and not contributing to beneficial Outputs?

With your thinking caps on, I really believe that some of you will be able to identify possible improvements as we move through this material. As we get further you may decide to eliminate some of them and/or add different ones. In addition, at some point you will want to 'test' your ideas to see if they work as expected or not.

What do I mean by that? I mean that all improvements have to be validated first on the basis of logic and reasoning. Then they have to be validated in a practical way which means they are tested in the 'real world'. The real world is on the practice field and batting cages. Nobody should change their hitting process without significant understanding as to why and supported by testing. This applies to young players as much as the pros. You have a lot invested in the hitting process that you now have. That should not change without thorough mental and physical testing to be sure that you are convinced the new process will be better. Once you are convinced, perfect the execution. Only then are you ready to use it in games.

Focus on Simplification

As we listed the questions on simplification above, did you come up with any ideas? If you did, that is a good indicator that you are comfortable with change. If you didn't, you may be more inclined to see our development first.

Now we will test your willingness to consider change on the basis of logic and reason. We will physically test it later if we pass the 'logic' test.

During the set up and in the ready position, where does every hitter start their bat? For simplicity, I'm going to describe it as sticking straight up. That is, the far end of the bat is toward the sky and handle is pointing toward the ground. Thus the bat is perpendicular to the ground. It is best to not get hung up on minor variations of this. The key is that it is generally that way.

Now I ask you, where does the hitter hit the ball? A simple question, right? Everyone had better answer that the hitter hits the ball with the bat essentially parallel to the ground at home plate or slightly in front of it. That means we have gone from the bat being perpendicular to the ground and now is parallel to the ground Is that wasted motion? Does that take extra time to execute? Worse yet, is that extra motion causing detriment to the key Outputs of the hitting process? We shouldn't worry only about the detrimental effects. We have to weigh them against any beneficial contributions to the desired Outputs. Those are simplification questions. In my opinion the answer is simply, yes. On a more detailed and logic basis, the answer is that yes there is extra and/or wasted motion there.

Your response may not have been so quick. It may be that you don't think it matters or some will say that the current way is required. Do you see what I meant earlier when I said we are going to push against your general attitude for change? If you aren't willing to look at *'all'* aspects of a process, you will limit the chances for improving it. You may be willing to limit it, but I am not. My objective is improvement and I'm not willing to let preconceived ideas or past beliefs go untested. If there isn't justification from all aspects for each element of the process, it is a candidate for change and improvement.

In order to gain perspective, we have to address any concerns you have on my comment about a possible simplification. We haven't defined specifically 'how' we would make a change to simplify the process yet. I have only proposed a conceptual change that we could simplify the process on the basis of logic. Let me clarify the issue. If all hitters hit the ball with the bat essentially parallel to the ground, why should we start with the bat perpendicular to the ground? I hope you are curious at this point. Curious as to where this will take us on the path to possible improvements.

Here is the proposal. Let's lower the bat in the starting position to the middle of the strike zone and be parallel to the ground. That places it closer to the plane of the incoming ball. It reduces the motion needed to deliver the bat to the ball. That is clearly reasonable and logical. I realize it isn't the final answer but this needs to be on our list of possible improvements.

I believe there are a series of concerns that I can anticipate that you have. Here is at least a partial list of concerns:

1. We have always done it that way.

2. If we don't start that way we will not have any bat speed.

3. We have been taught that we need to have a downward swing motion in order to put backspin on the ball so that it will carry further.

4. It doesn't feel comfortable in any other position.

Let's address each of these. If you have other concerns, maybe the comments provided here for the other concerns will address them.

Change—Required to Achieve Improvement

'We have always done it that way' is probably the #1 reason and response to not change. Process improvement (PI) folks get that response from the current users when looking at a process for improvements. Think about that for a moment as a justification for not considering change. If we didn't ever make a change to what has been done before, we would be back in the dark ages. We have essentially changed everything we do. The only reason we have advanced is because one or more people have been willing to try a change to improve it and they found it was better with the change and that becomes the new 'norm'. In my opinion, it would be much harder to find something that hasn't changed. How we cook, the tools we use to do home improvements, the equipment used in manufacturing, the cars we drive as well as changes to all the roadways, etc., etc. A car that is over 25 years old is classified as an 'antique'. The speed of change is even getting faster. 25 years ago we essentially didn't have cell phones. Now we are almost to the point that cell phones that aren't 'smart phones' are considered 'antiques'.

Let's go a little deeper on this. In all of the changes we have experienced over the years some are products and others are processes. Way back when I asked you to think about changes in sports and to think in terms of both products and processes, I suppose that the product changes are easier to identify than the process changes. I expect the same here. Try this to help focus on processes. Instead of thinking about the changes to cars, think in terms of changes in the process of how we get to work, travel for work or pleasure. In many cases the change in the process was largely due to a change in a product. In many respect they go hand-in-hand. The changes in how we get to work might be: (1) we ride a bike because we need the exercise, (2) we bought an electric car due the excessive mileage and fuel cost, (3) we take public transportation because it is now available and wasn't before, or it is cheaper, (4) we go a different path because they put in a new freeway that saves me time, (5) etc. These should clarify there are just as many process changes even though they may not be the 1st ones to come to mind?

What about changes to travel? Do you still travel on the same plane as 15 years ago? Do you still make the reservations the same way you used to? How do you coordinate your schedules now (computers, cell phones, etc.)? How do you track whether the planes for departure or arrival have changed? How many more ways are there to get frequent flyer miles now? How many more ways are there now to 'use' your frequent flyer miles than there used to be? Whoever heard of a 'cell phone parking lot' at an airport 10 years ago?

Another way to view this is that behind every product improvement, there could be many process improvements. Many new products could have never been made if there wasn't a change (improvement) in how it is made. Think about the golf club (driver) for a moment. Changes to the process of making the materials, the design process, the equipment for the design process. The processes to make semiconductor circuits have changed dramatically over the years to make cell phones and iPads available. Look at the cost of 'memory', circuits and displays used in all the electronic devices like computers, phones, digital TV (no more analog!), HDTV, 3D-TV, etc. These are just not possible without huge changes to processes so the products can be changed (improved).

Where are you now on 'that is the way we have always done it'? If you still want to stick with that, I recommend that you stop reading. If you can't deal with that level of change, there is no way you will grasp or be comfortable with some of the things we have in store for you. This is not being negative. Change is a big challenge for many people. They just don't like it and do everything they can to resist it. They sometimes will actually take steps to prevent it. That just won't work in the world of PI. I may do this too often, however let me remind you that Einstein believes we are insane if we expect better results without making a change.

Concern #2 Needs to be Addressed

This concern is a little more complex. It involves theory and beliefs. Beliefs often exist regardless of whether there is sufficient data to support them. Theories and beliefs can often be more like concern #1. They believe it to be true because it has 'always' been that way. You should know by now that we are not going to accept that without assessment. The 1st

thing we do is look at what data there is to support that belief. Frankly, we couldn't find any data. That puts it a little more in line with concern #1.

On a logic level, we can ask ourselves where the power for generating bat speed comes from. Does it come from the bat traveling down to the hitting zone or does it come from the hips? Think hard about this before you answer.

There is no doubt that gravity provides some force on the bat to pull it down to the ground. Since we are not swinging the bat down, that force is working against us rather than for us. The only energy or force provided to move the bat toward the ball is from the arms, hips & body of the hitter. From this it is reasonable to conclude that since we have not changed the methods of the hips or arms, there is no reason to think there is any change in the forces that provide the bat speed or momentum. We are just proposing that the bat start down instead of up and the hips and arms will bring it forward in the plane of the ball.

Keep in mind that we also need to look for possible detrimental issues. The hitter needs to hit with the bat in the strike zone. It is very conceivable that the process of bringing the bat down may involve muscles and processes that affect the Accuracy of the bat-to-ball placement. That is a serious issue! That detriment must not be set aside and forgotten. If there is no or at least minimal impact on the bat speed by lowering the bat and a possible impact on the Accuracy, this may need to be tested in the batting cages.

Addressing Concern #3

For a short name, let's refer to this concern as 'downward swing'. I won't argue the physics that back-spin on the ball will cause it to travel a little further (all other factors being equal). However, there is a huge price to pay to get it.

Essentially all the books out there teach the ready position of the bat perpendicular to the ground. Most of them also state that the bat should be in the same plane as the ball for as much of the swing as possible. Contradiction, right! They never apply any additional reasoning to combine those 2 statements and see the contradiction. If our ready position has the bat already down and close to the plane of the ball, our proposed change will eliminate the contradiction.

Some actually state the need to have the downward swing and reference the back-spin factor. Though the physics of the backspin adding to the 'carry' of the ball is valid, none of them address the far bigger issue, timing. A downward swing plane seriously reduces the hitter's chance for success.

To consider this timing issue precisely, we would have to calculate the difference in the amount of time available for a connection of the bat and ball. The amount of collision time will be different if the planes they are traveling in are at an angle of incidence of 5 degrees as compared to the angle of 15 degrees. Until that is done, the precise number will not be available. My expectation is that amount of time for contact will decrease exponentially as the angle increases. That is a huge problem! It is very detrimental for the hitting process outputs. As a result, the need for a 'downward swing' absolutely fails the logic test. The ball-spin physics are OK, but the physics and math of the impact on timing is horrible.

That is the big price I was referring to above. Lost connection time is expensive to a hitter. We already covered that the hitter is getting punished for being close (Axiom #4). This issue makes it much harder on the hitter to time the swing right. As such it is detrimental to the desired outputs of the hitting process and logically dropped.

How Important is the Swing Plane?

When thinking back many years ago, I realize that I experienced what might be the best way to convey that a 'flat' swing plane (not downward) would be best. When my son (Kevin) was only about 1.5 years old, he could hit. How's that for a shocker! I caution you though, don't be too fast to claim I am crazy. It will be a good example of not having all the right data. If we jump to conclusions without supporting data, it could and usually will result in a wrong conclusion.

One day Kevin and I were on the living room floor. It was very typical dad, son and family time. He was sitting there with one of those little tiny plastic bats that you get at souvenir shops. It was only about 12 or 14 inches long and very light weight. I was about 6 or 7 feet away from him with a relatively small plastic ball. Kevin was a ball freak. He loved balls. Any kind or type was fine with him, but he liked to have one with him all the time. At that point I did something for which I'm not sure why. I rolled the ball toward Kevin a few inches to his side. He very casually slid the bat across the floor and hit the ball. He was facing me in a sitting position (feet and legs were pointing toward me). The bat was on the ground and pointing away from him to his right (right-handed). When I rolled the ball to him so that it was going to pass him on his right side, he slid the bat horizontally across the floor and hit the ball back in my direction.

At first I thought this is just a fluke. There is no way he (at that age) could be 'hitting'. Well I decided to test the 'fluke' aspect and rolled the ball to him again. He hit it again and it was right back to me. It wasn't a fluke. I proceeded to keep rolling the ball and he kept hitting it back to me. He not only somehow knew to swing the bat; he also had a sense of 'timing'. Without the timing, the ball would have gone in random directions. As a dad, that was really cool! Since he was a ball freak, we returned to that activity regularly.

It wasn't until I was working on the hitting process that I realized how important that episode was. The importance was the swing plane. He wasn't strong enough to stand and hold a bat to swing at a pitched ball. If I had tried to pitch (standing) the ball to him (standing), he would have been unable to hit anything. However, in this controlled environment, where the bat and the ball were in the same plane, he could hit. Let that sink in a moment. When the bat and the ball were both in the same plane, even a very small child could hit the ball. This is a big factor to consider in the improvement process.

Moving on to Concern #4

This one is very closely related to the 'I don't want to change' concept. It is natural to resist change but it is never justified with the wrong reasoning. Of course you would feel uncomfortable doing something a new way if you have been doing it for 5, 10 or more years. That in no way justifies that the old way is better. You and anyone interested in improvement will always be up against that issue.

Let's be sure to put this concern in perspective. It may be good to review the 5 Axioms again. There is no luxury of doing what we want. We must make the appropriate changes to get any significant improvement. If we don't, Einstein has classified us. I want to make sure that if you have a concern about a change in the hands and bat position at the start of the swing for comfort reasons, that you aren't placing emphasis in the wrong place. Focus on strategic changes for improvement.

Comfort with change, both mentally and physically, come with utilization. The reason we are comfortable with something is because we have done it a lot. I expect you have made some improvements in your life that have resulted in your belief that changes can lead to good and better results. If you have not been able to achieve any improvements, it will continue to haunt you. I don't want to be harsh here but that isn't going to be the basis for the rest of us to not test the ideas we develop. If you are going to wait until everybody else is doing it, then you will not benefit until you do. Keep in mind, I wouldn't be writing this if we didn't find any benefits. This book would not be here if the changes we found didn't improve the hitting process. Leading the way is not in the psychological makeup of everyone. You won't be barred from trying or using it in the future by not going forward now. It is not in your best interest to continue something that can be shown logically to not be the best way. Not trying it because it doesn't feel comfortable is an excuse not a valid justification.

What If You Have a Different Concern?

It is possible that you have a concern that wasn't listed. Here is my suggestion on what to do in that situation. Look back at the information that was presented on the other concerns. Do any of those comments apply to your concern? If so, great. Another possibility is that we are going to cover a lot more info as we go forward. That additional info might provide the answers you are looking for. If you still have a serious enough concern, contact me.

Consolidation of Inputs on Simplification

Though my 'method' of introducing these concepts to you may be different than you have experienced in the past, don't fret. As we continue, you will gain comfort in the process and flow of information. It is good to have some understanding of why you should consider simplification.

Due to its common occurrence in PI we often find that a small change in a process can result in major improvements. This statement applies to all aspects of our lives as well. One reason to say that now is that we are not necessarily looking for major changes in order to find major improvements. As I said before, my objective is to find improvements to the hitting process and I'm willing to consider anything. My belief is that we will be able to make relatively small changes resulting in big improvements.

I doubt you will have viewed the swing process (a subset of the overall hitting process) in the way I will describe. When a pitcher delivers a 90 MPH fastball, it will take about 0.4 seconds to leave their hand and arrive at home plate. How many hummingbird wing flaps did you count in that split second? I have to ask you to stay more analytical with me. Since the hitter has to decide whether that particular pitch is the one to hit they typically need at least half of that time (0.2 seconds) to decide whether to swing at that pitch. That means that the swing process has to be executed in 0.2 seconds. That's not hard to calculate, however it is a little harder to conceptualize that the whole swing process has to be executed in 0.2 seconds. Keeping in mind that the hitter is punished for being close, it adds to the reasons to consider simplification.

If we can improve the swing process by 0.04 seconds that gives the hitter a 20% increase in the amount of time the hitter will have to decide whether that pitch is the right one. That's easy to calculate, but more difficult to conceptualize. Reduce 0.04 seconds and gain 20%. Does that sound like a small change that leads to a big improvement? Ask any hitter. If you had 20% more time to watch the ball before deciding to swing, would that appeal to you? You don't need to ask them; you know the answer.

Simplification vs. Accuracy

There is a topic we didn't spend much time on before. Our expectation is that changing the starting position of the bat (down to parallel with the ground) might also improve our most important Output in the hitting process (Accuracy). With the bat down, the body has to do less to get the bat to where the ball is. Not only is that a reduction in time; it is also a simplification that could increase the Accuracy. As stated earlier, when looking at simplifications, we have to consider their good and bad impact on the outputs. If we see a potential increase like in this case with no expected decreases, that is a change that we should consider.

Before any testing, the following info was assessed. I can't jump to the end. It is best if I tell you the process and not only the outcome. Of the folks I worked with on this, essentially all said they see the potential benefits (reduced time to execute and possible improvement in Accuracy). A significant majority but not all agree that the hitting process can be executed without any significant loss in bat speed. Essentially all are in agreement that an increase in Accuracy would produce more energy transfer. On a comparative basis the increased Accuracy and corresponding increase in energy transfer are more than enough to justify the logic side of the assessment. Conclusion–they would be willing to apply it in the real world (batting cages and practice field).

That should create a different perspective on why to look for simplification in the swing/hitting process. To me it did! It also gives me added confidence that with good, hard assessment, we can find an improved hitting process. We haven't gone that far and we already have a potential 20% improvement in viewing time, improvement in Accuracy and a corresponding increase in energy transfer. I'm very happy with that and we haven't even started looking at hard core improvements. At this point you should be seeing the benefits in not only the assessment process but also the outcomes.

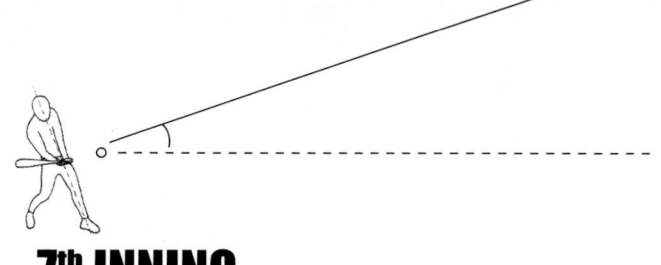

7th INNING
Focus on Additional Improvements

It is time to switch our focus from 'simplification' to 'improvement'. Although they have the same objective, the approach is a little different. Back in the 5th Inning we developed the understanding that Accuracy (bat-to-ball placement) is the most important Output of the hitting process. We now will use that as a key focus for improvement.

Conceptually, with accuracy as the most important Output, any significant improvements we can make to Accuracy without hurting the other outputs will be beneficial to the overall hitting process. With a hypothetical example I can give some added awareness. We don't have a way of calculating a numerical rating or percentage of Accuracy as compared to the other outputs. Let's hypothetically say that as the most important Output, it represents 80% of the Output. If that is the case, then a 10% or 20% improvement in Accuracy represents an 8% to 16% improvement in the process. That seems like a very worthwhile endeavor.

However, the Outputs are not totally isolated from each other. They have interactions. For example, improved Accuracy will undoubtedly improve Confidence. Changes that improve Accuracy will most likely improve Balance as well. We should not ignore these symbiotic relationships between the Outputs and vigilantly look as well for any detrimental relationships. Combining this hypothetical example with common sense, it is clear why effort spent on improving the primary Output is advantageous.

In order to best assess what improvements we can make to Accuracy we have to study it closely. If possible we want to isolate the largest contributors to Accuracy. How do we do that? I'm sure you would have chosen the same as we did: study videos of the hitting process on as many players as possible. There are a vast number of games and broadcasts on TV. We gathered videos of MLB games, MLB Post-season & World Series, college games & College World Series, and Baseball Tonight broadcasts. This involved thousands of hitting process episodes. We were looking for consistencies, inconsistencies and any elements that shed light on what produced better Accuracy.

Note the difference in looking randomly for what can be improved as compared to looking specifically for items that affect the Outputs. This targets our thinking. We can be more disciplined in looking at changes to Inputs or the process that will improve the good Outputs and/or reduce the bad ones.

Had I never played the game, this would have been more difficult. My personal experience as a player and coaching younger players was a major benefit in this situation. The experience coaching was more advantageous. Having seen the struggles of young players to know what they 'should do' and how to 'execute' it along with 'eliminating variation' in their hitting process was enlightening. Bringing the knowledge of those experiences into this assessment was paramount.

What did all the videos show? We were able to see some things that were very consistent. We saw that when hitters got a good connection/energy transfer, characteristically they had little or no head movement (HM). This was significantly different from when hitters didn't get good connection/energy transfer. In this aspect we are essentially using energy transfer as a representation that the bat-to-ball accuracy was good. Is that reasonable? Of course! How could you not have good energy transfer and not have good bat-to-ball accuracy? The data clearly showed us that there is an extremely important connection between HM and Accuracy.

From a contrary view point you can have good bat-to-ball accuracy and *not have* a well hit ball. Characteristic of that is when there is good Accuracy but low bat speed. It typically occurred when the hitter was 'fooled' by the pitch. Their stride was not matched to the pitch. They were way out in front of the pitch with weight shifted forward and unable to rotate their hips and generate any bat speed. Periodically that was seen in the videos. This represents when some of the hitting process was not executed well to deliver the other outputs even though the most important Output, Accuracy was delivered. Obviously, an undesirable process. The process we develop should be more robust to guard against untimely weight shift or prevention of hip rotation. And this should in no way deter us from seeking no HM to achieve improved Accuracy.

Now back to the good and desired process. The videos clearly showed that those hitters with great results had one thing in common. They had no head movement (HM). This was not only the consistent element of the hitters that had great Accuracy and excellent energy transfer. Those same great hitters when they executed the hitting process with higher HM produced an undesired output. This means HM is a differentiator between good hitting and bad hitting! The data showed it differentiates the good hitters from when they execute their hitting process well with no HM and when they execute their process poorly with HM. That is a key to problem solving.

Detour For Problem Solving

There is another process improvement (PI) tool that hasn't been mentioned yet. It is a tool for problem solving (PS). Thanks to Nakazawa I was introduce to it. Audaciously he pushed me to read the book 'The Rational Manager" by Kepner & Tregoe. PS is a key segment of their book. They too understand the need for application of scientific methods and rational thinking by managers to solve problems. They give many examples of when not used, managers implemented solutions only to find they didn't eliminate the problem. Again, Nakazawa's mentoring led me to a valuable tool.

It has been found by PS experts that in order to be sure you have the 'cause' of a problem identified; it must pass the IS/IS NOT test. To some extent we are trying to solve a problem. We are trying to determine the cause of inaccuracy in bat placement. In that situation, we should be able to use this test to determine if we are on track.

This test works best if there is only one cause of a problem. When there are multiple causes, it gets more complicated. It doesn't make the test not work; it just means that you may have to work a little harder at breaking down the test conditions to isolate the multiple causes.

The IS condition is when the 'cause' of the problem results in the 'problem' being present. Similarly, the opposite must be also true to pass the test. Thus, if the proposed cause of the problem is not present; the problem is also not present. This represents the IS NOT condition. If the cause IS present then the problem exists and if that same cause IS NOT present the problem doesn't exist.

In our application, we would have to use the negative viewpoint. The problem would be defined as poor hitting process. The cause we are testing is 'too much

HM'. If in the videos too much HM resulted in the problem (poor hitting process) that would meet the IS condition. Similarly, if the videos revealed that no HM also resulted in the problem disappearing that would meet the IS NOT condition. Our study of the videos did validate those findings and both IS and IS NOT conditions were met.

That is a significant aspect of our findings in the study of the videos. We found that when the hitting process was Accurate with an effective energy transfer, there IS no significant HM. We also found that when the process was inaccurate, there was significant HM (IS NOT). This makes it very clear that no HM is a key part of bat-to-ball Accuracy. We want to improve Accuracy. It makes perfect sense that we will need to look for ways to reduce or, better yet, eliminate HM. This is an added confirmation of our findings being significant to improving the hitting process.

How Do We Eliminate Head Movement?

Data crunching by video analysis showed us that head movement (HM) directly relates to Accuracy. That gives us a major focal point to look for improvements. We now have a harder task. We have to find ways to improve it. As with anything difficult, we should try to break the bigger task or objective into smaller pieces. We need to look at the hitting process as a series of elements. I suppose you can determine what some of those elements would be. Here are some of the ones we identified:

1. Set-up or ready position
2. The step or stride
3. Moving the hands downward
4. Moving the bat downward and parallel to the ground
5. Moving the bat toward the hitting position
6. Using the hips to generate power in the swing process

You know by now, I want to take a look at these one at a time. That gives us a basis to match our understanding of how they may be affecting HM on an individual basis.

We have pretty much already worked on #1. It was part of the simplification assessment. If you recall, we left that assessment with a possible simplification of moving the hands and bat down to be parallel with the ground at the middle of the strike zone while in the ready position. We also believe those simplifications will reduce the execution time and contribute to improved Accuracy of the process. They all passed the logic assessment. We left those as items to be tested.

Does the Step or Stride Contribute to HM?

As #2 on our list, I am going to ask you to stand up and look in a mirror (full length if possible). Now mimic taking the stride that a hitter in baseball takes. The size of the stride varies. It may vary from 6 inches to 12 inches depending on the player, their 'preference' and coaching. You should be able to do this without watching your feet. For the right assessment, you should be facing the mirror and the stride should be parallel to the mirror not toward the mirror. I want you to watch in the mirror and assess if your head moves.

I am sure that at least 99% of you saw significant HM. I didn't say 100% only because there are folks that won't see it the same way as most. The fact is, it's essentially impossible to take a stride and the head not move.

Now if you are really sharp you are saying, yah, but... All the videos we studied were of players that 'took a stride'. Those of you that thought of that should pat your selves on the back. You are really 'thinking' about what is being done here and that is *great*.

When we studied the recorded videos to understand this we found that the players that had no HM were doing a couple different things. The vast majority of them fell into two groups. First, was a group that was taking the stride well before the pitch left the pitcher's hand. The second group was moving their front leg forward in the stride motion, but was not shifting their weight forward onto the front foot. Let's consider simulating those two methods while watching in the mirror.

The first group is not realistic to test because you aren't actually seeing a ball being pitched to you and you can't simulate the timing of the stride. This should give a major clue to the problem with taking a stride. Timing relative to the pitch is already a problem and we haven't even considered the difference in timing needed for a fastball compared to a change-up.

Most of you should be able to simulate the second group. That involves having most of your weight on your back foot so that you can lift and stride the front foot forward. If you try that a few times, you should be able to simulate the motion of moving your front foot forward but not the rest of your body and especially not your head. It is tough to do this without moving your head. As a result you will sense with this method as well as with the first group that there could be a way to improve this part of the process.

This little exercise allows you to see for yourselves what can be done to meet our objective. Our objective was to see if we can find ways to eliminate HM. Your first reaction to that might be—just do what those players did. Since there were players that had good Accuracy and energy transfer, what they did may be a good path to follow. That is a very reasonable thought. However, I am going ask you to think a little deeper on this before we move on. Go back and read those last few paragraphs again and use critical thinking of what is really happening. Keep in mind, if we keep doing the same and expect different result, we may be insane.

Now that you have thought about it, let's see if you came to the conclusion we did. Our idea or improvement is to not do what either group 1 or 2 did. Why? Einstein's definition of insanity was a big influence. Group 2 is a better clue than group 1. Group 2 really didn't take a stride. They moved their foot forward but actually didn't take the stride. Now apply that to group 1. They really didn't take the stride either. They did it before the pitcher delivered the ball and thus they were making the motion but doing it before the rest of the swing was being implemented. That exemplifies the significantly detrimental impact the stride has on our Output: Timing.

What is common to both of them? Let's call it the *'Un-Stride'*. When it really comes down to it, neither was actually taking the stride. They were un-striding.

Maybe unconsciously they knew that taking the traditional stride was detrimental. By trial and error or the school of hard knocks, they had learned what you have learned with PI analysis, that HM is detrimental and it needs to be eliminated. So I ask you to seriously consider. If neither group is actually taking the stride, what is the best way to eliminate the HM caused by the stride? You should arrive at the same conclusion we did. Eliminate the stride!!

That took us a while. Wow, that is very fruitful! We have found and eliminated a significant source of HM and its detrimental impact on Accuracy. This was a bit of a revelation; it felt very satisfying. I hope you felt that too. You have 'walked' through an analysis with us that has brought us to an 'ah-hah' moment. Good PI tool application brings about many ah-hah moments. It is fun to be scientific and apply our findings to the real world. Often we find something that was puzzling before now makes sense.

Let's Group Elements #3 & #4 Together

There is a method to our madness in doing this. We already mentioned doing both 3 & 4 in the 'simplification' section of the 6th Inning. They were reasonable to us then, and still are; moving the hands down to the middle of the strike zone and positioning the bat parallel to the ground in the ready position are simplifications that would reduce the time to execute a swing. It may also help other swing process outputs as well. On a logic level we also believe we will get less head movement (HM) and its corresponding improved Accuracy in those changes. We will move toward testing the results of those proposed improvements.

Don't Pressure Me to Break Tradition!

It is time for the 7th Inning Stretch! You aren't going to get me to break such a tradition. Who's going to lead us in 'Take Me Out to the Ball Game'?

Let's Group Elements #5 & #6 Together

When looking at these two elements or movements, we see that they are somewhat similar. Only the arms, hips and body can bring the bat toward the ball. We have shown the data and solid reasoning to eliminate the stride to increase Accuracy by eliminating HM. We need to maintain those gains as we consider how to move the bat toward the incoming ball in connection with no stride. We have a good working point.

We must keep a focus on our objective (eliminate HM) while we execute the movement of the bat to the ball. We have already established that Accuracy is the most important hitting process Output. Our analysis then showed that the most important improvement we can make to Accuracy is by eliminating HM. After considerable evaluation of how to complete the swing, we decided to take a different approach. We decided to take an 'end-game perspective'. That is, where do we want the swing process to end? We decided that by looking at the end of the swing and working backwards; it would give us a different perspective.

That new perspective required us to define the end-game of the swing process. I can best describe it by the hundreds of photos in many books by players, coaches and hitting gurus that show a position typically called the 'hitting position'. Characteristically they all show essentially the same position. There also seems to be desire of the photographers (magazines and newspapers) to catch the hitters in the 'hitting position'. In Gwynn's book (The Art of Hitting), there was one group of 4 pages that had at least one such picture on 3 of them. Many of your minds will immediately conjure up an image of the 'hitting position'. Especially those that have and are studying the hitting process will know this position. I want you to get that image and then we will work backwards. Take a look at Fig. 4 and see if it matches the image in your mind.

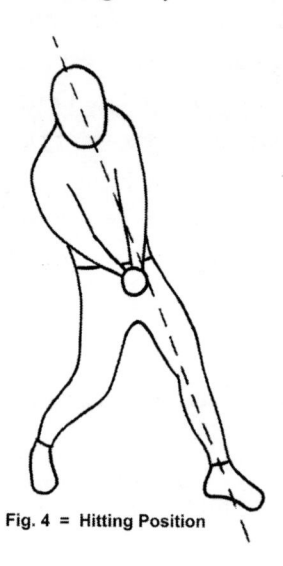

Fig. 4 = Hitting Position

Working Backward From the Hitting Position

Some key terms or elements of the hitting position must be established: (1) a stiff and straight front leg; (2) the arms are fully extended; (3) the bat is parallel to the ground, perpendicular to the incoming ball and slightly in front of home plate; (4) the hips are 'open' (more explanation later); (5) the back leg is bent with the weight balanced over both feet; and (6) the body (torso) and head are in a straight line; the same line created by the straight front leg. I need you to capture that image and completely imprint it in your mind. We are going to use and build on that crystal clear image. It will be important for many references going forward in our analysis and development.

Use of the end-game method of starting with the hitting position and working backwards, is a choice of approach. The hitting position is not actually the final position of the hitter after the swing is completed. It is sequentially closer to the middle. However, it is the end of hitting portion because after contact, what is done has less impact on the desired Outputs. Our primary focus is on the portion of the swing from the ready position until the hitting position.

We should keep in mind the simplification questions we asked earlier. Those questions are: (1) where are we duplicating, (2) what steps are insignificant to the final Outputs or are a waste of resources, and (3) which steps are possibly contributing to detrimental Outputs and not contributing to beneficial Outputs? We can keep it simple and avoid detrimental effects on the desired output (Accuracy), by keeping those in mind.

What would be the simplest way to get back to the proposed 'ready position'? Our simplification view of that would be to do two (2) things. First is to 'un-open' the hips. Second would be to retract the arms back close to the body. We really want to keep all the other items pretty much as they are. We want it to be simple in the changes as we go backwards. Those 2 main changes would leave the bat parallel to the ground but back in the ready position. With hands retracting, you now have them back in the ready position. We were surprised, maybe as much as you, by how simple that was. Simple is good.

As an added viewpoint of simplification, we would always view it beneficial to have our starting (ready) position as close to the hitting position as possible. That means we have to do the littlest amount of change to get back to the desired position (hitting position) with the least amount of steps, effort, etc. If we do that, we will have the simplest hitting process and reduce the time to execute it. As you will recall from our previous work, that will give the hitter more time to decide which pitch to hit. That is good, maybe even great!

Keeping Accuracy in Focus

Simplification is good as long as we keep the other key outputs from being detrimentally affected. Now we need to assess what we can do to achieve the movement from the ready position to the hitting position with Accuracy {meaning no head movement (HM)}. Staying with my desire to keep you focused on the process, can you think of any way to achieve that movement in a simple and direct way? Work it through and see if you can create an idea or method. Turn the page when you are ready.

Development and creative thinking are never easy. Experience is helpful. We decided to create an 'axis'. The axis was chosen because it will help us achieve all our current objectives in this part of the assessment. In case those are not clear, let's restate them: (1) Simple motion from ready position to hitting position; (2) no HM; and (3) maintain all other outputs at desired levels. The simplest motion we could perceive was to 'pivot about the axis'. In the ready position, the axis is created (Fig. 1 & 2). The stiff front leg, torso and head are all in alignment (axis). The hips would start the pivotal motion. As the pivot continues the torso joins in which then causes the arms to start moving forward, yet still close to the body (Fig. 3). As the motion continues the shoulders join the pivotal motion about the axis. During the pivot, at the right time, the arms extend to deliver the bat to where the ball is (Fig. 4). At that point, the hitter is now in the hitting position. The hitter will then continue with the follow-through (Fig. 5).

Let's clarify the details of the 'axis' we created. The axis (though imaginary) is functionally precise. If you could see it, it would look like a pole that starts above the hitter's head. It continues down through the hitter's head, torso, stiff front leg and out through the front foot and into the ground. Fig. 1 & 2 show the ready position (front and back views) with a representation of the 'axis'. It might be helpful to envision this by going back to the image we created to show the hitting position (Fig.4). The axis is in the same position. Now put the pole in place without moving anything on the hitter. That pole is symbolic of the axis. The hitting process is to pivot in the sequence just described about the axis from the ready position to the hitting position and then follow through to the end.

Fig. 1 = Ready Position (back)

Fig. 2 = Ready Position (front)

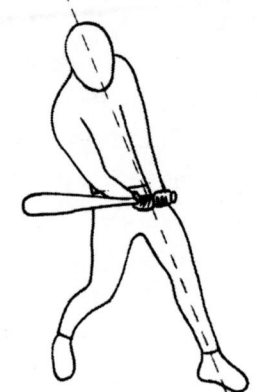

Fig. 3 = Start of Pivotal Swing

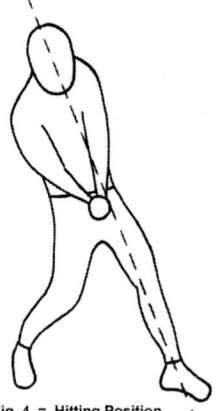

Fig. 4 = Hitting Position

Fig. 5 = Pivotal Swing Follow Through

Pivotal Swing

The sequence described allows the hitter to move from the ready to hitting position in the simplest, most direct and powerful way. Keep in mind there was no stride. The need for Accuracy of the bat-to-ball placement demands that we have no head movement (HM). These 2 changes, no stride and creation of a pivotal axis, are major contributors to our objectives. Since the head is also on the axis, it should not move.

In case you didn't catch it, we just described the Pivotal Swing®! We have taken a lot of thought and analysis to get here. Your concentration and assessment should unite you in kindred spirit with us. You demonstrated willingness to challenge the status quo and look for improvements. My expectation is that you were able to anticipate some of the items we uncovered. When you didn't, the added info we provided led you to what we developed along the way.

Other Benefits to the Outputs

If you remember from our past assessments, we need to consider the impact of these elements on the other outputs of the hitting process. We need to assess and be confident that the elements and motions we have selected do not create detrimental impacts on the other outputs of the hitting process. Our focus was to get from the ready to hitting position in the simplest and most powerful way while generating no HM. In order to decide to go further and test what we have developed, we must pass the logic test and confirm our belief that these changes will have beneficial impacts on the other outputs. At the very least we don't want to see any detrimental impacts.

Let's quickly go through each of the outputs. Accuracy was the focus of that effort and we are confident on a logic basis that we have improved it. Energy Transfer is directly linked to Accuracy. We saw the best Energy Transfer in thousands of videos studied when the HM was the lowest. Our developed method has eliminated HM so it should also be great for Energy Transfer as well as Accuracy.

As for Timing, we can see excellent benefits. Elimination of the stride provides major gains by eliminating the associated HM. In addition, there are major issues with the timing of the stride and its impact on timing of the swing. Since the hitter doesn't know the speed of the pitch, guessing whether it is a fastball or change of speed, ultimately creates Timing problems that the Pivotal Swing® eliminates.

Confidence can only be assessed by the hitters after they try and use the method sufficiently. Balance and Execution Time are still on the list.

Our end-view approach to working backwards helped to minimize any wasted motion and improve Execution Time. Simplification of the motion to bring the bat to the ball is beneficial. This should be the fastest Execution Time of any swing giving more time to decide which pitch to hit.

We haven't really spent much time on the output 'Balance'. Our logical assessment of this new method is that it will dramatically improve Balance. By eliminating the stride, we made a major contribution to increasing Balance. Without any stride, the timing difference between a fastball and an off-speed pitch is eliminated. The hitter can concentrate on the pitch longer because they don't have to time a stride or shift any weight, which are detrimental to Accuracy, Execution Time and Balance.

Balance, in our assessment as a key Input & Output, gains stability with these changes. With the feet a little further apart, we gain stability from the start. When the hitter is pushing on the stiff front leg with the back leg and holding the axis in place to pivot around, there is no weight shift with stability and Balance as the benefactors.

With those assessments of the impact of the changes on the Outputs, we have passed all the logic tests. In comparison to Lao Tzu's journey of a thousand miles, we took that single step and began. By breaking down this huge endeavor into smaller more manageable pieces, we assessed their individual and corporate impacts on the hitting process. All segments of assessment, both simplification and improvement, have logically led us to the Pivotal Swing® method. With the pure logic found in the assessments there is emphatic belief that real world testing is not only appropriate, but we would be remiss in not doing so. We anticipate the Pivotal Swing® method will deliver significant improvements. Only testing can give us more data to assess. Using Nakazawa's advice, we can 'let the data make the decision'.

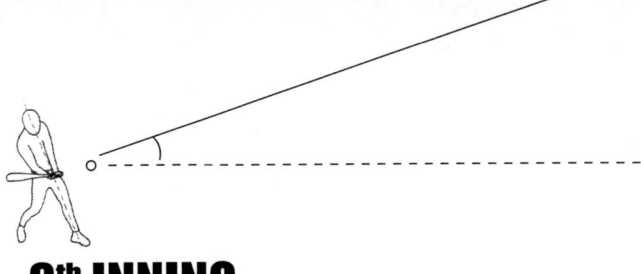

8th INNING
Dramatic Test Results

Our testing showed over 30% improvement in 4 high school players that had between 8 to 10 years of experience. All 4 players improved between 21% and 42% with an average of over 30%!!

We chose them because we don't have any personal links to MLB players. This book should create needed links to higher level players and additional testing. Without access to professional or college players, we still needed to proceed with testing. Being frank with you, I didn't think they would welcome me without having the contents of this book available. I tried to imagine what it would be like to introduce the Pivotal Swing® without the book. It seemed like an insurmountable task. A quick trip down memory lane will also remind you of the comments made earlier about the different reactions to change. We will get all of them. However, the benefits of the Pivotal Swing® method are far too solid to be overlooked for the wrong reasons. Rather than debate all the potential issues, let's move on.

Testing warranted using experienced players with enough experience to minimize their variation. Younger players with too much variation in their hitting process would conflict the data. A very significant point here is that this testing was done after only 10 to 15 minutes of training. They were not able to fully execute the method as planned but with what they could absorb and execute in that short time, they were able to generate on average over 30% improvement. The expectation is that their improvement would increase dramatically with more understanding and emphasis on the specific elements of the Pivotal Swing® method.

"What do I expect the results will be with the professional players?" you might ask. That is very easy to answer. All of the analysis both video and by personal observation was of MLB and college players. Therefore, I expect the results to be as good or better. I say that for 2 major reasons. First is the training time of those tested. With more time and understanding of the elements and how to execute them, the higher level players will benefit as much or more.

Second is the level of player and their commitment. Professional and college level players have a higher level of commitment to both having the best process and executing it well. In the case of the MLB players, their pay (maybe even their career) is dependent upon it. In the case of college level players, many aspire to play in MLB and will need to have the best process to get them there.

Younger players should all benefit because it will eliminate the primary causes of poor results (variation) in their current hitting process. The added benefit is that the earlier they start using the Pivotal Swing® method the more comfortable they will be with it. Part of comfort comes from time of usage.

As you recall from earlier in the book, the desire and objective of a process improvement (PI) effort is to find core level PIs. When that is done, 'anyone' that uses the improved process will get better results than they did with the old process. The Fosbury Flop in high jumping is a great example of that in sports. We believe the Pivotal Swing® method is a core level improvement. The best indicator of that is that all 4 players tested, improved. Had only one or two improved, the view of this would be different. With all 4 experienced players improving, significantly, that is a very good indicator of a core level improvement.

In order to assess that completely, we need to find MLB and college level players to test it. Obviously that has to be done in the batting cages and practice fields. I believe the best way to do that is by getting this book out. Without the contents of this book to show the higher level players *'Why'* this method is better and worthy of their consideration and *'How'* to execute it, their lack of 'willingness' might be justified. With this book, any lack of willingness is not justified. Does that mean every player will be ready to test it? Heck no. Change is not easy for many and almost impossible for some. What I hope for is that some great players will see the logic & analysis and be willing to test it with a limited license agreement. Those interested should contact me at Roger@PivotalSwing.com.

1st Level Testing

The dramatic test results I described to you above will be referred to as 1st level testing. It will be helpful for you to know how that testing was measured. It was focused on assessing our most important Output of the hitting process (Accuracy).

This too will require a little visualization on your part. We broke the way the ball left the bat of the hitter into 3 types. Type 1 was a line drive hit. Keep in mind that this is a range, but it is easy to judge when a ball is hit 'well'. Those were Type 1 hits. Next we'll describe as a Type 2 hit. These can be described as long fly balls and grounders (one bounce at most to reach an infielder). The last category is Type 3. The Type 3 would be classified as a pop-up or dribbler. Combining this with our assessment of Accuracy, it is easy to relate that Type 1 hits were when the hitter had the best bat-to-ball accuracy. Similarly, the Accuracy decreased as the type increased. We didn't track what might be viewed as a Type 4: a miss or foul-tip. The reason for that is that hitters get punished for being close. Since the hitter gets punished less for Type 4 conditions, we didn't track them.

Since Type 1 is the desired output of the Pivotal Swing®, in the testing of the method we are looking for more Type 1s. Improvement would be classified as moving from a Type 2 to a Type 1 or from a Type

3 to a Type 2. Since the hitter improved the accuracy of bat-to-ball placement if they hit a type 2 instead of Type 3, that is an improvement.

We measured the Type of hits for all 4 players using their existing method or hitting process. We did this on 25 hits for 2 players using live pitching and 2 in the batting cages. We then gave them the explanation or training on the new method. The coining of Pivotal Swing® had not taken place yet; at that time it was the 'new method'. That took only 10 to 15 minutes. Combining all the time for explanation and experimenting with the new method, there was less than 15 minutes before we started the testing of the new method. Keep in mind their execution of all the desired elements was incomplete. That is fully understandable with such a short implementation time. However, they clearly were executing a large portion of the new method consistently.

We then measured again the type of hits they got with 25 hits using the new method. In comparing the number of Type 1, 2 and 3 hits, we found that all 4 players had more Type 1 and 2 hits and had fewer Type 3. That means they moved some up from Type 3 to Type 2 and Type 2 to Type 1. The range of improvement was 21% for the lowest and 42% for the highest. That was an average of over 30% for all 4 players.

2nd Level Testing

Let me follow that by saying that we do not have enough testing yet. Yet is the big word here. A main purpose of getting this book published is to create linkage. We are looking forward to testing by a number of you. That will be our 2nd level testing. Please keep in mind that this method is under the control of Patent Pending. Please also review the 12th Inning. We will get into the details of the legal factors involved with a Patent Pending process.

Anyone interested in using the method needs to review the limited license agreement very carefully. The purpose of that is not to scare anyone away. It is only to control its usage. Younger players have less control issues. We want to keep close track of professional or college level players that want to use the Pivotal Swing® method. In future releases of the book, we want to include the test results of those who acquire a license to use it. Please contact me at Roger@PivotalSwing.com to join the effort of—How *'You'* can Help Improve the Game of Baseball!!

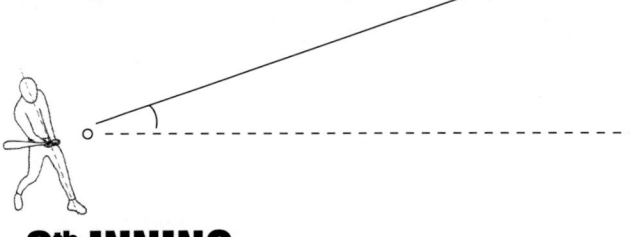

9th INNING
Who Will Benefit the Most?

We actually don't want to be selective in trying to define who will benefit most. I'm reluctant to single out a group because we are confident we have a core level process improvement. As such, *any* player using the Pivotal Swing® method will get better results. However, from a more realistic viewpoint, some players will need it more. They will not only need it more, they will be more 'willing' to bridge the 'change issues'. We can establish who they will be?

Anyone in a Hitting Slump?

First on our list would be players that are in a hitting slump. Since this method takes the player back to pure fundamentals of the swing and is focused on both eliminating the time to execute and improving the Accuracy, it will work very well in getting a player out of a slump. Reducing their time in a slump is paramount. As they do that, they will be developing the skills needed to execute the new method well.

Let's reason this a little further. If the Pivotal Swing® helps get them out of the slump, why would they want to switch back to some previous method? This is one of those moments when a player or a coach needs to eliminate the emotions and focus on the logic. In some ways it seems odd to even mention this. It is hard to argue with the logic. The problem is that it's not easy to remove emotions and just think logically. There is a tendency to fall back to what is comfortable rather than what is best. If done correctly, at some point the Pivotal Swing® method will be the 'comfortable' place and that is when the player has fully embraced both the reasons 'why' the method is better and they have also achieved the supporting results. That is the foundation of confidence and long-term results.

Who's Not in the Starting Line-up?

2nd on the list of candidates that will benefit most are players that are currently not in the starting line-up. They need something to break the coach's view of their ability to contribute to the team. Although there are other ways, hitting is very high on that list. If the player is also a specialty player, with an improved hitting performance they may be able to bump a player that is a little better fielder but not as good of a hitter.

As players advance to higher level teams it gets harder to break into the line-up. Many players have always been a starter and they don't actually know what it feels like to not be in the line-up until they get to higher levels of play. Some players find this at the college level. Others don't actually find this 'wall' until they get to the professional level. Only the elite superstar escapes this situation. Everyone else has to deal with the decisions on how to improve their performance to differentiate themselves from other players.

Let's not be too simplistic here. Most superstars have to work to stay 'on top' of their game and their competition too. Some folks have more ability (God given talents: eye sight, strength, quickness, coordination, all of which may be described as kinesthetic intelligence) than others. They too must have the best process. It is an age-old battle between the less gifted that work very hard to develop skills and processes that allow them to compete with those that may be a little more 'gifted' than they.

This will be a case in which early adopters of the Pivotal Swing® method can surpass those with a little more ability. They may be able to get a head-start on some that have more ability and then 'stay' ahead of them in the development of the Pivotal Swing® method. There is going to be development along the way. We will be working on the next level improvements to the Pivotal Swing® method. Those that get started earlier will have an advantage that may be hard to catch.

When a better process produces more consistency, a new 'plateau' is reached. The stability of that plateau becomes the foundation upon which more refined and complex process improvement tools can be used to take the process to the next level of performance. That is exciting! We may then be seeking a new era—the .500 hitter!

Don't lose sight of the general aspect of processes. If a better process is developed, anyone that uses the better process should get better results. The Pivotal Swing® method may fit better with some players than others. In the long-run, that will be visible statistically. In the short-term, the early adopter of the better process has the advantage.

Specialty Players

Next or 3rd on the list of who will benefit most are players in the line-up for reasons other than their hitting. They are position players that are valuable to the overall team effort and not in the starting line-up because of their hitting performance. These players can benefit tremendously by improving their hitting. They can solidify their position or possibly increase their pay. If a player is a .220 hitter and moves up to a .255 hitter, that is significant. That could mean hundreds of thousands of dollars in a player's contract.

Though players can't overlook the pay issues, it is often less interesting to a player than getting to play. If you aren't in the line-up it is hard to continue developing or improving (especially hitting). It's much harder to contribute from the bench.

You probably know what positions are available to players that aren't the best hitters: center field, 2nd base, short-stop, catcher and pitcher. The value (measured in contract dollars) of these players will improve dramatically if they are also better hitters.

Aging Players

What an interesting category! Some players have reached an age that doesn't allow them the same flexibility or strength they once had. These players could use a boost. The Pivotal Swing® process is the most robust process. That means it will produce the best results for the widest range of variables (inputs to that process). Precision and accuracy become even more important. Higher bat-to-ball accuracy will give an aging player the best possible energy transfer possible.

The wisdom of an older player can be extremely beneficial when it comes to understanding and executing the best process. Wisdom can also be displayed in choosing which process and data reflects the best process. As we have stated, the best process is the most robust and aging players will benefit from using the most robust process. They may not hit as many home-runs but .400 hitters will always be welcome in the line-up.

Young and Amateur Players

This is a big group. The group involves everyone from Pee-Wee, Little League, Pony League, High School and Club teams. The biggest improvement in young players involves reducing the variations in their swing process. Unfortunately the variations possible are far too diverse to list here. A very important step for young players is to select the best process possible. Then they should focus on executing it perfectly with each and every swing. Gwynn and other top hitters heavily emphasize the need for consistent execution and development of muscle memory.

Variations in executing the chosen process result in variations on the outputs. When a hitter has too much variation in the execution of their hitting process, it is more difficult to determine if the process is the problem or their execution.

The best process for young players should create the right conditions for avoiding the detrimental elements of hitting. Some of the detriments to prevent or eliminate are: lunging, pulling your head, swinging too hard, extra movements, etc. That doesn't mean it won't take time to develop comfort and ease with your chosen method. Comfort and ease come with clear knowledge, mental imaging and lots of practice.

We spent a lot of time earlier to show that the Pivotal Swing® method was the most robust process. That is the key reason it's best for young players. The most robust process will deliver the best results over the widest range of input variables including the skill of the hitter. Rest assured that if you are using the most robust process, you will get better results than doing exactly the same execution with a less robust process.

Robustness is a design feature of the process and independent of execution. Neither good nor bad execution changes the robustness, only the outputs of the process. Obviously the best results are obtained from the best execution of the most robust process. The Pivotal Swing® method and this book were developed so that you don't have to do development on your own. You only have to read, assess and decide. First decide if it is the best and most robust. Then decide if it is the process you are going to use. At that point you are ready to focus on execution and to do so perfectly every time.

The above comments are focused on the process aspects. A very important factor for young players is the broader view of physical and mental development. Amateurs should focus on overall strength and skill development. The pros are doing it. Doesn't it make sense that you should too?

There is a large controversy over young players committing to one sport and concentrating all their effort on it. Though that has some merits, I believe the detriments are worse. Young player are still developing. A well rounded athlete is much more desirable in my view. Skills from different sports help with overall development. Even though it is the dream of many young players to go all the way to MLB, that isn't usually decided at age 12 or 15. There's no more requirement for that decision to be made at 15 than a business career. Pointing in a direction is fine. Locking in at 15 or less is not good for young athlete's overall development. As one gets older, the paths get narrowed down and visibility increases on which path is best. It really bothers me when kids in high school are being pressured to focus only on one sport. I was fortunate enough to get to play football, basketball and baseball for multiple years. I cherished all of those opportunities and challenges. I wanted that for my kids. However as with others, our kids were pushed toward committing to only one sport. OK, I'll get off my soapbox.

Let's focus on the Pivotal Swing® method and its application to young players. As you saw in the development process, we sought the most robust process. The overall design included structure to aid in Simplification, Balance and Accuracy that will help younger players reduce their variation by preventing lunging, eliminating head movement and non-contributory movements, etc. One of the primary reasons young players have trouble generating good results is they have more variation in their hitting process.

Here is another bold statement. The Little League team that embraces the Pivotal Swing® method the fastest and most effectively will win the next Little League World Series. The robustness of the process will overcome so many of the difficulties young players have. The robustness of the process will be more evident at this level of play. By eliminating a lot of the variation the younger players have, their hitting process will be much more accurate. This is a significant advantage at this level and is enough to move teams up in the brackets. Strong pitching is always a factor. However, better hitting will prevail!

The amateur's Limited License is very simple to acquire at www.PivotalSwing.com. Amateur players and coaches can get started quickly and easily.

Fitting In With Existing Coaches

Earlier in the book there were two key statements. First was that we were confident we could find relatively small changes that would produce big improvements. Second was that those changes would not be inconsistent with many of the elements being taught by existing coaches and gurus. This is a good time to address those more specifically.

Our development was bathed in simplification and focused on improvements. Though some may argue, the changes to improve the process are relatively small in the overall scheme of the whole hitting process. Only you can make the final judgment on whether you view the changes as relatively small. Had we suggested that every player hit on the opposite side of the plate or that every hitter should start on their knees, those would be classified as radical changes and not consistent with any current teachings. Instead, we summarize the Pivotal Swing® method changes as: (1) Lower the bat to be parallel with the ground at the middle of the strike zone in the ready position. (2) Eliminate the stride. (3) Form a 'pivotal axis' with a stiff front leg which continues upward to include the torso and head. (4) Pivot about that axis, starting with the hips, to deliver the bat to and through the hitting position. Whether you consider those changes as big or small is somewhat moot. The development is done and the real decision is whether you agree with the logic, assessments and conclusions at a level of deciding to test them.

The second point was that our changes would not be radical or inconsistent with many of the elements being taught by existing coaches and gurus. In some respects that requires you to be versed on what those folks are teaching and coaching. Most of us don't have access to ask questions of the authors, MLB coaches or the gurus. However, we do have the coaches of the teams we play for or local to us. One way to assess the compatibility is to ask them. Keep in mind; the only way they can answer that question effectively is for them to have read the book as well.

Let me offer another perspective and point of assessment. In Gwynn's book (The Art of Hitting) he writes, in the Chapter called the Hitting Clinic, about 'The Swing'. He says, "The swing makes the most sense to me when I think of taking the knob of the bat to the ball." He goes on to explain that in more detail along with a reference to a picture in Williams' book (The Science of Hitting) of Hank Aaron that perfectly exemplifies his point. I agree completely with him.

That warrants additional explanation. During the 'pivot about the axis' in the Pivotal Swing®, incorporating Gwynn's point or method is perfectly compatible. As the hitter starts his swing with his hips, with the arms and hands still close to the body, the hitter can use Gwynn's method. Along with the pivot around the axis, the hitter can start pulling the knob toward the incoming pitch to align the bat with the ball. While continuing the pivot about the axis, the rest of Gwynn's inputs including the follow-through are compatible with our new method. Examples are good. This clearly shows how the concepts of Hall of Famer Tony Gwynn are compatible with the Pivotal Swing® method.

Competitive Advantage

Competition is what this world is all about. Often parents want to shield their children from this, but eventually, especially in sports the real world gets revealed. That is a big reason parents like to see their children get involved in sport. They learn many good life lessons about such things as hard work (physical & mental), discipline, education and competition. In many aspects of life we are seeking to gain a 'competitive advantage' that will set us apart from the crowd. Everyone wants to win the 'World Series' or be a 'Champion' in some endeavor. Those that choose to implement and perfect the Pivotal Swing® will have a 'competitive advantage'.

Some won't see the logic and benefits until others have already done so. My dad used to say, "The early bird gets the worm." The longer a person waits for the general acceptance to grow, the lower the 'competitive advantage'.

You Baby, Yes, You!

The final group of those who will benefit most is *'You'*. At the risk of being too repetitive, we'll say it again. This is the most robust process available. Every player will benefit from the most robust process. The sooner you get on the cycle of learning and executing it, the sooner you will be leading the way to the new .400 era.

We just finished the bottom of the 9th inning.

However, the game is not over.

Folks, it looks like we are heading into extra innings!

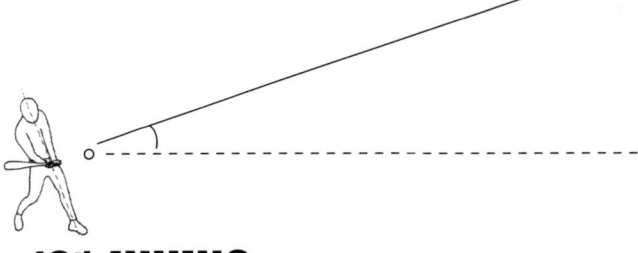

10th INNING
What Is the Impact on the Game?

The baseball industry is prolific in the number of stats published. I'll use some of them to show you things I doubt you have considered. Most have some idea on what the top batting average has been or who hit the most home runs in a year. You may even know some of the less publicized stats like the number of strike outs for the 'big hitters' or the number of stolen bases for the fastest runners. Many of those stats are interesting and pertinent to various viewpoints about the game.

I suspect many knew we haven't had a .400 hitter for a long time without knowing it was Ted Williams hitting .406 in 1941. To me that stat is much more than significant. Even more important is the question *'Why?'* In a simplistic sense, I could easily state that pitching methods have improved more than hitting methods. In a general sense that is at least arguably true. It was definitely part of my motivation to seek understanding of 'why' and 'how' the hitting process could be improved. As stated earlier, I view this not as the result of great pitching but more as a failure of hitting.

There are some harder questions. I suspect that only a handful of folks will know the answer to any of these. The answers to them have significance when we consider the impact a new hitting process can have on the game. Over the last 25 years, what do you think was the batting average for the top team of both the National (NL) and American Leagues (AL)? If we combine both leagues it comes out real close to .281. More specifically the AL average is above .284 and the NL right at .277. That shouldn't astound anyone. I'm not going to address why the difference, maybe the designated hitter rule.

Now, over the last 25 years, what do you think was the batting average for the bottom team of both the NL and AL? This one may be a little more of a surprise to you. Would you believe .247? That is a bit rhetorical but interesting. Individually there was less differences between the leagues on this one with AL over .248 and the NL just a little under 246. Roughly that would be an average of about .247.

The lowest difference between the top and bottom teams (last 25 years) in the NL was 16 points. In 1987 the top team was .268 (Mets) and the bottom team was .252 (Dodgers). The same comparison for the lowest difference for the AL was in 2004 when it was only 24 points (Angels .282 and Devil Rays .258).

What is amazing to me is the *difference*. That says that on the average, the difference in batting average between the top team and the bottom is only 34 points (.034). That really amazed me! How about you? That told me 34 points would change the game of baseball! With that change a team can move all the way from the bottom to the top. That is a big deal!

You may not be aware, but that has happened (well close) to some teams. There are 30 teams in MLB now. In 2005 the Tampa Bay Devil Rays were the 3rd highest batting average with .274. In 2006 they fell all the way to the bottom (last place, 30th) with a .255 average. That was a only a 19 point drop but a huge impact in their standing. A similar fall was the Chicago White Sox in 2006 were the 4th highest average with .280 yet in 2007 they fell all the way to the bottom with .246. That is a 36 point drop.

Looking in the opposite direction, a climb from the bottom to the top, we also see examples. In 2005 the Minnesota Twins were 23 out of 30 teams with a .259 average. In 2006 they rose all the way to the top with a .287 average which is a rise of 28 points.

What can we assess from these numbers? 1st and foremost is that a 30 point change can move a team from very low to very high and the reverse. The 2nd point is that none of those that rose from near the bottom to high up have done so by a hitting process improvement (PI). They did it by changing the players, hitting coach or maybe even the manager. That is more in line with Moneyball (Billy Beane's method) using stats for decision making. It is not a change caused by any hitting method PI.

Let's take a side-step for a moment. Do you remember the comments made earlier about a 'core level' process improvement (PI). If we apply that here we can see some interesting outcomes. If the Pivotal Swing® method (or any other PI) creates a core PI of 30 points or more, the game will never be the same. In the past teams have moved up from very low to very high as shown by the examples. If a team or teams adopt a new method that is fundamentally a better process, they will have an advantage.

How do you feel about the sub-title of the book now? When you 1st saw it, I'll bet there was a question in your mind. There shouldn't be any doubt now. Any doubt about 'will' it happen should now move to 'when' will it happen.

What about your involvement in the use of this knowledge? There's a *'You'* in there! Where are you going to fit into this 'new picture'? Are you a player, a coach or influencer? Are you comfortable with change? Do you lead the way with change or do you tend to follow what everyone else does. That is just a matter of whether you adopt the change earlier or later. There will be a learning curve and those that start earlier will be further up the learning curve. Even the early adopters will need time to perfect the Pivotal Swing® method.

The Pivotal Swing® method should truly be classified as a small change, not a large one. What we have developed is somewhat small modifications to existing methods. Because the changes are small modifications, they are something that players can test and use in a relatively short period of time. The 1st level test was done with less than 15 minutes of training and understanding.

A Small Change Can Produce a Major Improvement!

Let me reinforce the earlier comments on this topic. There are a number of viewpoints. Let me show you some of them.

The article called 'Return to Form—Veterans Bouncing Back From Lost Seasons' was posted on the CNN Sports Illustrated (cnnsi.com) website on May 5, 2000. It has a clear description of this concept. In this article, Hall of Famer Ozzie Smith states "Sometimes is just takes a small change to make a big difference." In the article he describes how Terry Mulholland, Frank Thomas, Derek Bell and Todd Hundley all made very small changes and got major differences in their baseball hitting or pitching performance.

The website HOOP BOOST (a blog) had a post from Bob Starkey on March 23, 2010. The blog states,"… It was frustrating for me. I quickly became the worst hitter on the team. I was embarrassed and didn't

know what to do, and then I remembered *Ernie Banks*....
Ernie played baseball in the 1950s, and he lightened his bat by 3 ounces. He went from hitting 19 home runs to 44 home runs—all because of 3 ounces! …"

In the Los Angeles Times on June 28, 2011 there was an article by Mike DiGiovanna about Mickey Hatcher the LA Angel's batting instructor. It relays the message of how he improved performance dramatically in Peter Bourjos and Mark Trumbo with slight changes. Hatcher helped Trumbo correct a slight upper cut in his swing and Bourjos to change his mind-set. He is re-iterating that very small changes in baseball methods can produce major improvements.

These examples are being used to reinforce the perspective that the Pivotal Swing® method is making relatively small changes that will produce big improvements. These articles are representative of many more that all convey the same message: small changes can produce big improvements. The more strategic and effective the changes: the bigger the benefits.

The last reference in the LA Times had a very interesting comment. It referred to changing the 'mind-set' of the player. Isn't that what Confidence is all about? That was our 3rd Output of the hitting process. We are always interested in any contributions to the hitter's Confidence. When the hitter is given a better process, they will have more Confidence they can produce beneficial results. It is not only a builder of Confidence in the individual players but also the whole team. That is the foundation of most hitting rallies. Any team that can generate more hitting rallies is going to win more games.

Is Baseball a Game? or a Business?

It is too simplistic to just say it is both, so I won't leave it there. What may separate or define the difference? Age would be one. The younger you are, the more it's a game. Perhaps the biggest differentiator is money.

Poker and Blackjack are just card games. That is, until you start betting money. In that comparison, when salaries of players or team management get involved, it is no longer just a game. It has transcended from a game to a livelihood. Careers are made and broken on performance. That applies to management as well as players, though we only hear all the hype over player's salaries and contracts.

Nothing said in this book will change the fact that it will remain both a game and a business. However there are some business factors that the book could influence. Dr. Kiemele mentioned this in his statement (Foreword). With Six Sigma deployment, generically process improvement, so pervasive in the Fortune 500 companies, why has the sports industry eluded its impact? Those of us that have been exposed have a pretty good idea: because ownership and/or management aren't asking the right questions. This is not meant to be critical; it is merely pointing out a difference. If the leadership never asks the question: how can this process be improved? Nobody is going to seek the answer. If they did ask that question but only of those in the 'inner circle', they may not get any answer different from what they have heard for years. You can surmise that neither I nor Dr. Kiemele was in that 'inner circle' because you know that we would give them an answer they have never heard.

Though to me it seems odd that Six Sigma and PI haven't invaded professional sports or baseball, it could just be lack of information. Maybe it has and we just haven't heard about it. If so, you can bet I will hear about it. A more likely scenario is that by lack of awareness of the methods and potential, it never became part of anyone's 'to do' list. There is a good chance that will change.

Is the business of baseball radically different than other businesses? They too have many processes involved with operation. We might benefit by segmenting the 'baseball business' into two groups of processes. Let's refer to them as 'player performance processes' and all the rest as 'general business processes'. This segmentation is just chosen because these two segments appear to have characteristics that require different handling for our purpose.

Addressing the general business processes first, let's ask if they are significantly different than the general business processes of other industries or teams. Generically we can answer, no. The baseball industry faces very similar business process issues as the rest of the business world by staffing, organizing and managing their operation. They recruit the best management and staff possible like most others. They may be different in that they may never have sought an executive or manager with process improvement credentials. You can be sure that Motorola, GE and many of the Fortune 500 companies specifically have that as criteria for the leadership they seek.

The baseball industry can get by (status quo), as do other industries, as long as nobody innovates or develops a better process. When that happens, the status quo is disrupted. Depending on the process, that disruption can be radical.

Comparatively, consider the video industry. Blockbuster developed some better processes for the handling and distribution of home videos. They put a lot of mom & pop video stores out of business. They grew fast and did very well financially. At least they did for a while. What happened? They have nearly been put out of business by Netflix who developed an even better process. You can bet that isn't the end. If Netflix doesn't continue to innovate and improve their processes with the new technology being developed, they too will be trumped by the next better process.

Baseball teams and the industry need to stay ahead of their competition too. Billy Beane's "Moneyball" concept caused some turmoil within the industry. What Beane and the A's organization did was develop a new process for selection of players. It was very successful. The industry has adapted, at least for now.

Are Player Performance Processes Different?

It appears that player performance processes are different than most general business processes. One difference is how variation is handled. Another is the pursuit of improving them may need different tools. Since every process is different, the tools must be chosen based upon the conditions in which that process is operating. It is not uncommon to apply PI tools for personnel performance processes in precision manufacturing environments, maybe not so different than the intricacies of professional sports performance process. There may be more flexibility to change the tools, equipment or machinery available to those people than for a sports player. That doesn't prevent the application of the tools, it just sets the parameters in which the PI tools are chosen and applied. If applied properly, there is no process that cannot be improved.

In most companies, variation in their general business processes, adds cost to their bottom-line, resulting in reduced profit. If a player hits .250 rather than .300, the team doesn't lose money. They can still market their team and generate sales, independent of the player performance. Consider that although baseball is an industry, they are part of a larger industry—entertainment. As long as they deliver entertainment at the level of their marketing plan, they may be able to thrive.

Remember we concluded earlier, baseball is both a game and a business. If a player doesn't perform, they can change the player to maintain the business. That works under two (2) conditions: there are sufficient players and nobody develops a better process. If they ran out of players to bring in when the performance warrants it, the business model would fail. Hence the farm team system.

The second condition is more complex. If a better method or process is developed, the balance of the overall system is jeopardized. The team leadership can no longer replace the player with a 'similar' player. The new method has created 'new' players. There are ways to stabilize the balance of the system, but it can cause some turmoil during the adaptation period.

This overall business condition of the baseball industry is not the primary purpose of the book. It is appropriate to mention these factors without trying to conclude everything the baseball industry should be doing. Player performance processes (hitting as one of them) is the primary purpose of the book. Introduction of the Pivotal Swing® method is going to impact the game/business. Whether it follows the description above remains to be seen.

General Pursuit of Process Improvement

If and when an organization decides to pursue process improvement (PI), the question of who should or could do it, gets asked. There is no required method to reach a conclusion. I highly recommend that it start at the top. You may recall comments earlier in the book that if the pursuit is not led from the top, it hits too many road-blocks and has dramatically less chance for success. Some key leadership members need to be indoctrinated on how it all works and what all the large companies with successful deployments have done. This creates an environment in which leadership and management will then 'ask the right questions'. Those folks can then lead the effort.

I don't want to try and turn this book into a deployment manual for PI. Dr. Kiemele and Air Academy Associates have already written those books. I do want to mention a few things that should be beneficial to those that are reading this. Expanded awareness is beneficial to everyone.

When an organization pursues PI, one thing that it should do is look at the same or similar processes outside or in other companies. If something better exists, the first step is to not 'reinvent the wheel', but rather use what is already available. Later steps, using that as a stepping stone, can be implemented to make the next level improvements. This book fits into that category.

When there isn't a better process available, the leaders need to determine who will be the right person or people to be trained and lead the efforts. There are two groups of people that are good for inclusion: insiders and outsiders. Insiders are those people most involved now with that process. They bring benefits and detriments to the effort. Beneficially, they already know a lot of the steps, what is good as well as what is bad, and often have ideas for improvements. Detriments should also be considered. Their past may hold them back on developing the best improvements for fear of peer issues or an array of other fears. Their views of possibilities may be more limited and more influenced by taboos.

Many efforts to improve require a project team and are a good way to include outsiders. In this way, detriments of any individual can be overcome by selecting team members that can counter-balance the effort. All members should either have a good acceptance for 'change' or at least be coached on it. A project loaded with 'naysayers' is not going to succeed.

Serious consideration should also be given to including 'outsiders'. Their benefits are: wider perspective, not trapped in old or ineffective traditions, and not held by 'group-speak'.

Some words of encouragement to everyone. If you get a chance to participate, take it. Better yet, seek out the opportunities to join such an effort. Many of the processes in businesses have been improved by folks that the company didn't view as a high level 'change agent'. They were regular folks. The difference was the acquisition and application of PI tools and methods. Many of those folks did attain major recognition from the leadership of the company, division or group they were part of. The organizations benefitted from those efforts. Sometimes the benefits were radical. The most interesting ones to me were the ones achieved by the least likely folks, by seeking and finding very simple changes that created huge benefits. We saw many of them inside and out of Sony.

Who Gets The 'Low Hanging Fruit'?

A common element to those unique situations was: first application of PI methods to that process. There is a common term for those initial benefits in the PI world.

Those folks were fortunate to capture the 'low hanging fruit'. Just as it sounds, any of you that have picked fruit from a tree (apples, oranges, pears, cherries, etc.) have found the low hanging fruit is the easiest to capture. Once the low hanging fruit is gone, the harvester must then seek other tools (ladders, poles, etc.) to capture the next group of fruit. You guessed it! The hardest fruit to capture is always at the top of the tree. That doesn't mean that very good and beneficial improvements are not found in those applications as well. It is just that more sophisticated PI training and tools are needed. It may also require a person and team that are much more effective at organizing their knowledge and efforts in order to bridge organizations. It typically requires leadership that understands both process improvement and change management. Many organizations have difficulty accepting and implementing changes, even when they are best for the organization.

I am fortunate to have been the one to capture the 'low hanging fruit' on the hitting process. It is often a person outside, not the user of the process being assessed that takes on the challenge of improving it. That is partially because they see it a 'different' way. However, a big factor is that an outsider is more willing to challenge the 'traditional' thinking. Tradition is a huge contributor to ineffective processes.

Don't misunderstand me on tradition. Some traditions have resulted in tried and proven processes that are great. More than likely they have changed over time to be 'hardened' (like in the manufacturing of steel) into the great method and tradition that remains today. Family traditions are examples. Hold onto them! The world is changing all around us.

However, most traditions will have to change to adapt. Yep, traditions are processes too. Pictures at a family gathering are a great tradition. Just look at how that has changed over the last 10 years. We now have digital cameras, video sharing via Skype, picture and video sharing on Facebook, etc. Wow! I'm in PI shock! Take a quick look back at all the processes that had to change for that great tradition to be what it is today.

Beyond Impact On The Game

Above I gave some words of encouragement. They were directed at the general readership. However players may feel a little left out because it will be a while before any teams form player performance process improvement projects.

Some encouragement for younger players and young folks in general is important to me. You will face very interesting challenges in the coming years. Challenges present opportunities to those who are prepared. Pick your interests and passions and pursue them.

You may have missed a very subtle point. Opportunities arise for those who are prepared. To be prepared you must seek education, knowledge and understanding not just in reading and learning but also in the application of science, math and technology. Learn the basics and then expand. Process Improvement tools and methods are part of expanded learning. In my opinion, every high school student should be taught the basics of PI. Businesses need people to think and apply these types of tools on a daily basis.

In the pursuit of your passions or interests, get involved and then seek ways to make it better for you and others. In some cases you will be lucky to find low hanging fruit. In other cases you may need to join or form an improvement team. Don't wait for someone else to find the next level improvement. You can do it!

"Knowledge has become the key economic resource and the dominant, if not the only, source of competitive advantage."

—Peter Drucker

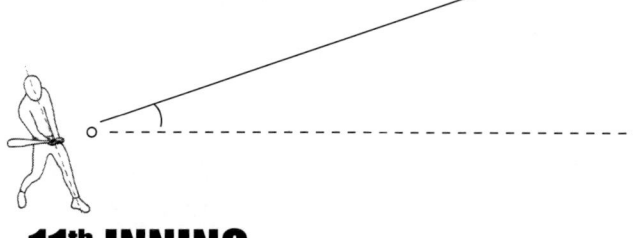

11th INNING
Clarification of the Pivotal Swing® method

As we continue in the extra innings, we need to hit some more line-drives! Reviewing all the key elements of the Pivotal Swing® method will solidify both the images that need to be in your mind as well as the functional execution. I want to create actionable motivation. How is that different from motivation? It's the 'get out of the chair' and 'do it' motivation as opposed to 'think it's a good idea' motivation. If you read the book and think it's great, that's motivation. If you put all the new knowledge to work for you, that's actionable motivation.

One thing that will move you to actionable is clarity. It's much easier to execute a process that is clear. A second item is solid 'mental images'. If you have a series of pictures in your mind, they will flow together into a full mental image of the process. Third on the list is belief or confidence. There are two aspects to this: confidence in the process and then confidence in your ability to execute it. When we get done, your images will be so clear that you will be executing the process in your dreams. Better yet is that you will be anxious to get out and hit some line-drives.

During Innings 5 through 7, we focused on how the Pivotal Swing® method was developed. This Inning we'll focus on the Line-Up/Roster of benefits. We have 9 heavy hitters in our line-up.

Batting 1st: Better Bat-to-Ball Accuracy

Batting 2nd: Simplified Swing–shorter execution time

Batting 3rd: More Time–to see the ball

Batting clean-up– Better Balance

Batting 5th: Dramatically reduced Head Movement (HM)

Batting 6th: Short Training Time–to get significant results

Batting 7th: Compatible–with many elements coached now

Batting 8th: Excellent 'slump' preventing and busting characteristics

Batting 9th: Confidence—as needed skills are developed and tuned

Who's the MVP of the team? As any good coach or manager would say, they are all valuable and contribute to the team in their own ways. If really pressed for an answer I would have to say Accuracy. As we focused on improving Accuracy, we found ways to, simplify the swing, reduce execution time, eliminate HM, have better balance, etc. This will be more evident as we review them individually.

Better Bat-to-Ball Accuracy

Most managers have some key criteria for their lead-off hitter. Those criteria typically include: fast runner, smaller strike zone, and most important a high on-base percentage (OBP). Our criteria includes more line-drives. Accuracy is the combination of many things built into the Pivotal Swing®. We have shown you that the most important Output of the swing process is Accuracy. It is directly related to Energy Transfer. When the hitter is punished for being close, we need the best Accuracy to get the best Energy Transfer.

We have to look beyond some of the key coaching inputs to better understand their meaning. How many times have you heard: watch the ball, don't pull your head, keep your head down, or stay in there? These are all contributing to the coach's belief that one or more of these things are reducing your Accuracy. How many times have you heard: focus on your bat-to-ball accuracy? I never did in the 13 years I played. That doesn't mean they didn't intend it; it just hasn't been a clear focus.

Other members of our roster are contributors to Accuracy. It isn't a standalone characteristic as with other heavy hitters on the roster. Simplified Swing and Better Balance are major contributors to improved Accuracy. We'll review those in a few moments in more detail to see how they add to improved Accuracy. At this point, improved Accuracy and corresponding Energy Transfer are going to increase your on-base percentage as a good 1st hitter should.

Simplified Swing—shorter execution time

A primary purpose of the 2nd hitter in the line-up is to 'advance the runner(s)'. With Accuracy increasing your line-drives and on-base percentage, our 2nd heavy hitter comes to the plate with a benefit that will do just that. A Simplified Swing has few motions and is more direct to the ball. This will contribute to Accuracy as mentioned above. It will reduce the time needed to execute the swing. That creates the added benefit of more time to see the ball and decide if that is the pitch to hit.

Fig. 1 = Ready Position (back)

Fig. 2 = Ready Position (front)

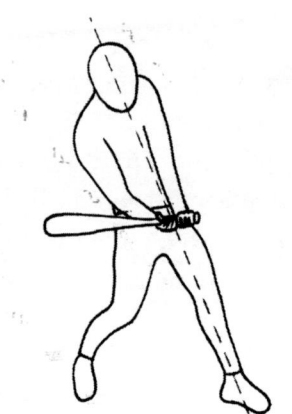

Fig. 3 = Start of Pivotal Swing

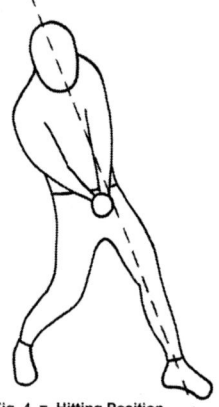

Fig. 4 = Hitting Position

Fig. 5 = Pivotal Swing Follow Through

Pivotal Swing

We'll use the figures or diagrams here to clarify. Take a look at Figures 1 & 2. These show the elements of the 'ready position' (stiff front leg, bent back leg, hands down to middle of the strike zone, arms against and hands close to the body). The dashed line represents the pivotal axis we created. They don't show that the back leg is pushing against the stiff front leg holding the axis in place and forming the strong foundation. The bat is lower and relatively parallel to the ground. By pivoting about the axis, starting with the hips, the hitter moves through the positions shown in Fig.3 and Fig. 4, after which the hitter finishes the follow-through (Fig.5).

The pivotal motion about the axis with the arms leaving the body at the right time for the bat to meet the ball is simple and compact. There are no wasted motions to use up energy or deter the Accuracy. This reduced amount of motion gives the hitter a Simplified Swing.

More Time—to see the ball

The Simplified Swing can be executed in less time. That gives the hitter more time to see the pitch and decide whether to hit it. With just a 0.04 second reduction in the swing time you are increasing the amount of time the hitter has to make that decision by 20%. It's a bit rhetorical to ask hitters if they would like to increase the time they have to see the ball better, because they will unanimously agree. If somehow you find one that doesn't, they may want to seriously consider whether baseball is their game.

Better Balance

As our 4th and 'clean-up' hitter, Better Balance steps up to the plate. Just like most #4 hitters, this hitter has a huge impact. As we already commented above, Better Balance supports the overall effort to achieve the best Accuracy on bat-to-ball placement. If the hitter is not in balance, there is a serious impact on the bat not being where it needs to be. Most likely it will also significantly reduce the energy transfer.

There are many aspects to balance. Let's consider off-speed pitches. Timing seriously complicates swings including strides. The hitter has to time it perfectly. Wow, how do you do that when you don't know if it is a fastball or change-up?! You don't. You have to guess. If you don't guess right your timing and Balance will be off. Yep, the only way to have the right timing and Balance is to guess what type of pitch it is. If you are wrong, oops!

Compare that to the Pivotal Swing® method. If you don't take the stride you don't have to guess, just use the extra time to see what the pitch is. When it is a good pitch execute the Simplified Swing.

The Pivotal Swing® method will have a huge impact on young ball players. Being out of balance due to an off-speed pitch is a very large cause of hitting failures. This element by itself could cause the result in the LLWS I predicted earlier.

As a part of the 'ready position' in the Pivotal Swing® method, the feet are a little further apart than a traditional stance. This creates a stronger foundation with better Balance upon which to execute the other elements of the swing. When the hitter is pushing against the stiff front leg and creating the pivot about the axis in Figures 1 through 5, the strong foundation enables the hitter to execute the swing motion without shifting their weight forward or backward. This better Balance contributes to the improved Accuracy and corresponding Energy Transfer.

Dramatically reduced Head Movement

As the 5th hitter in our line-up of benefits, we will 1st remind you of our findings. We studied thousands of videos of hitters throughout MLB and college. Use of technology for repeating and slow-motion studies was very helpful. It became clear as a result of all those videos that: the common factor between good and bad hits was the amount of head movement (HM). Interestingly, it was also evident that even a very good hitter that typically had low HM, would result in bad hits when their HM increased. This met the IS/IS NOT elements of problem solving.

Elimination of HM exemplifies a more robust process is better. A more robust process helps even the pros reduce the variations in the execution of their process. Heck if it was easy, it wouldn't be classified as the hardest thing to do in sports. The most robust process is going to help them achieve less variation.

Let me give you a new view on this. I'll give you a helmet to wear that has a laser beam shooting from it in exactly the same direction your eyes are looking. The beam is 5 feet long. That is about the distance from your eyes to where you hit the ball. If you then rotate your head 5 degrees in any direction, how far to you think the end of the beam will move? Would you believe roughly 5 inches!

What does that mean to a hitter? First is that any amount of rotation larger than 5 degrees is going to cause an even larger movement. Secondly, it should add major realization that you want to eliminate head movement (HM). Thirdly, your brain, body and the bat could easily be off by that amount or more if you have that amount of HM. 5 inches means that you totally miss the ball.

As you saw in the development, we created the pivotal axis. The head is on that axis because it needs to remain still. That means no rotation either. As we just described, a very small amount can translate into big variations. The Pivotal Swing® was designed to be executed more easily without moving the head. That is exemplary of its robustness.

Short Training Time—to get significant results

I gave the hitters in the 1st level testing only 10 to 15 minutes of training. I think that is a Short Training Time and they got significant results; all of them. As with anything, more training time is going to generate better results. The key is compatibility with their current hitting method. The modifications are not radical and that is why most hitters can adjust to it very quickly. Since the modifications are few and simple the time to implement them will be low.

A quick description would be: lower the bat, eliminate the stride, push against the stiff front leg, pivot about the axis and extend the arms to achieve the traditional 'hitting position'. Each player will have different issues and concerns for trial and implementation. That has to be done within their training and practice sessions. The amount of change can be very low and thus a Short Training Time.

Compatible—with many elements coached now

As players and coaches read this material, they should see that there are many details that don't need to be addressed because they don't need to be changed. Some steps like loading or coiling along with the stride have been eliminated as part of Simplification. With Better Balance and improved Accuracy from the pivot about the axis, there are fewer elements to execute. Many details of the hands, arms, shoulders, hips and legs are not being changed significantly. As a result, the Pivotal Swing® method will fit well with the other details coaches are working on with the hitters.

Excellent 'slump' preventing & busting characteristics

This is our 8th hitter in the line-up. It is not a normal 8th hitter. We expect a huge amount of hitting from this one in addition to its tremendous fielding skills. 8th hitters are quite often excellent fielders to off-set their less than robust hitting. The fielding for us is it 'catches' those in a hitting slump and turns them into benefits.

We explained some points about this benefit in the section 'who will benefit the most'. Hitting slumps have always been a conundrum for players and coaches. The causes and speculations of 'why' are wide in variety and linked to the details of the individual. Though confidence is a factor, there is often a swing fundamental that is being overlooked. Since Accuracy was found to be the most important Output, I'd look to our assessments and explanations in that area 1st.

The robustness of the Pivotal Swing® method is its basis as an excellent slump buster. It is designed to eliminate excess motions and simplify the swing process. That is a good path to follow when trying to get out of a slump. All the previous benefits are contributors to slump busting and prevention. Getting back to the basics is a common approach by many coaches to help a player get out of a slump. That's the way the Pivotal Swing® was developed. Thus it is an excellent way to both bust and prevent slumps. Sometimes a hitter's loss of confidence is imbedded in a slump which we will address next.

Confidence—as needed skills are developed & tuned

As our 9th hitter in our line-up, the aura of 'Confidence' is very wide and diverse. Nobody has a simple explanation of how one gets it or keeps it. Though it is illusive, don't give up pursuing it. Any amount you can accumulate is beneficial. In addition, all the comments written about it earlier are applicable here too.

If we get into the logic, we can make some headway. Our testing has shown that the Pivotal Swing® method is a core level process improvement. That means it is a more robust process. A more robust process will produce better results for anyone using that process. How will it not produce more Confidence?!

As with most processes, Confidence in and from it grows with practice and usage. Along with being Simplified, the other benefits will continue to produce better results. Confidence will grow correspondingly. The testing showed that significant improvements were made after only a short training session. That means additional development and skill training will also generate additional improvement and Confidence.

Details—Elements of the Pivotal Swing® Method

For clarity and precise imaging, here are the key elements of the Pivotal Swing® method:

1. Stiff front leg forming the lower portion of the pivotal axis.

2. Bent back leg.

3. Feet a little further apart than currently promoted.

4. Lower the hands to the middle of the strike zone.

5. Start with the bat relatively flat (parallel to the ground).

6. Form the upper part of the pivotal axis with the torso and head being on the same axis as created by the stiff front leg.

7. Eliminate the stride! Instead, push with the bent back leg against the front leg.

8. Use the 'pushing' as a method to eliminate other nervous, detrimental and un-contributory motions. (Keep your body 'quiet' and still.)

9. The 'push' is also holding the hips closed.

10. Decide if the pitch is what you want.

11. Unleash the power by releasing the hips to start the pivot around the axis. However, maintain the 'push' against the stiff front leg which keeps the axis steady and in place: no lateral movement and especially no head movement.

12. Do not shift any weight forward or backward, just pivot about the solid axis on the solid foundation.

13. As the hips continue the pivot, the shoulders join the pivot about the same solid axis, which has not moved.

14. Because the arms are against the body and hands are close to it, as the torso starts to pivot about the axis, they follow by remaining in place. They are moving toward the ball due to the hip, torso and shoulder rotation, not because they are moving away from the body yet.

15. When the hips, torso and shoulders have pivoted to where the bat is about ½ the distance to the ball, still parallel to the ground, you now have had enough time to decide what type of pitch it is and where it will be.

16. At this point you are adjusting and moving the arms and hands to line the bat up with the incoming ball (e.g., same plane as the ball).

17. If you were following Tony Gwynn's guidance, you would now be 'pulling the knob to the ball'.

18. As you continue the pivot, the arms extend from the body to deliver the bat to the ball in the 'hitting position' in great balance on the solid foundation that hasn't moved.

19. During the pivotal motion the body is 'quiet' yet powerful with hips unleashed and the pivotal axis solid without any movement.

20. The hips, torso and shoulders continue their pivotal motion around the axis after contact at the hitting position.

21. At this point, the hitter is past contact and other coaching inputs can be used from this point forward on completion of the swing or beginning to run.

Although I mentioned the inclusion of Tony Gwynn's 'pulling the knob toward the incoming ball', there are other coaching methods that can be included for details of the hands, or other areas not mentioned. There are a lot of details; however the flow will come easily with just a little practice. This is more detail than given in the level 1 testing. As pretty much any coach says, the hitter needs to have their method fully imbedded in their mind and muscle memory. Walking through the detail list is needed at the very beginning. After a little practice only a summary will be needed as a reminder. We have created one below. However, I would encourage you to develop a short list of no more than 5 items to place on a piece of paper and stick it in your pocket. The full detailed list should be in your bag. Review it consistently when you are heading to practice. You can rely on your summary list or the one below to remind you during practice or as necessary.

Summary—Key Elements of the Pivotal Swing® Method

When the details have been worked on sufficiently to create the mental images needed, a summary of the key elements can then be relied on in further development:

- Establish the 'ready position' that includes the solid foundation, lower hands and bat parallel to the ground.

- Form the pivotal axis and push against the stiff front leg with hips closed.

- Start the Pivotal Swing® first with the hips.

- Deliver the bat to the ball at the right time during the pivotal motion (about the axis) to achieve the 'hitting position'.

A periodic review of the detailed list should be incorporated in your regular routine and preparation for practice sessions. This list or your own version can be used as a quick reminder when the detailed review is less practical.

Actionable Motivation

We have given you the three items we said would create the actionable motivation mentioned at the beginning of the Inning. They are:

1. Clarity of the key elements in the Pivotal Swing® method.

2. Solid mental images by linking Figures 1-5 to the key elements.

3. The heavy hitter roster to build Confidence in the method and its execution.

If we could, we would do it for you, but we can't. We have presented to you the foundation of the sub-title of the book. It gives you both *'Why'* and *'How'* to do it. The implementation of the book involves *'You'*. Based upon your level of 'actionable motivation' you will either be a leader in the .400 hitter revolution or a follower. Only you can decide!

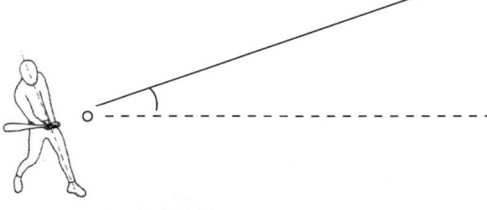

12th INNING
How Does Intellectual Property Fit Into this Picture?

I have decided to write and publish this before a patent is issued. I filed a utility patent application to protect the intellectual property (IP) rights of the Pivotal Swing® hitting method. Once the patent application is filed, the status of Patent Pending is granted. Patent Pending allows us to publish this but does not allow anyone to use the method without permission. I held off publishing anything just as a personal preference until now. Although not finalized with the Unites States Patent and Trademark Office (USPTO), until it is, the status remains as Patent Pending.

There are a number of aspects of intellectual property (IP) that are involved here. The USPTO is the government agency that handles IP. In July 2012 we were issued a Notice of Acceptance (NOA) on the trademark—Pivotal Swing. It is now a registered trademark and that is why the ® symbol is shown after Pivotal Swing® throughout the book.

Copyright fits into the picture as well. As you can expect this book is copyrighted. All the materials on the website are also copyrighted.

The more complicated aspect of the IP is the patent. 99 out of 100 people don't have any idea that you can patent a process. I was introduced to patenting of processes back in the 70s when I was a young engineer at Motorola. We were working on the development of CMOS microelectronic circuit processing. CMOS is now the predominant technology used for microelectronic circuits in all hand-held, portable and battery powered devices (calculators, PDAs, cell phones, laptops, etc.). The key is that I learned that Motorola was filing for patents on CMOS circuit processes and licensing them to other manufacturers. I had no idea then that it would become more important to me later (now).

The process here is to get each of these IP items in place as we proceed. With a patent, trademark and copyright, there will be much better control over the distribution and utilization of the Pivotal Swing® method.

Limited License

My disclosure of this method in this book is a choice. It is based upon a desire to get things moving. The patent process is long and complicated. With the Patent Pending status we can maintain control of the Pivotal Swing® method. The vehicle to allow and control its usage is a Limited License (LL). A LL is granted only to players via our website *www.PivotalSwing.com* or through contacting us. Amateurs can get it automatically from the website. College and professional players have different requirements. The best way for them is for their team to acquire a license. Under that team's LL, all players on the team will be authorized to use the method as long as they remain with that team. Their LL will terminate if they leave that team or the team loses the LL.

The Limited License for amateurs, for a small fee, allows them use of the method for 4 years or until the age of 18 or graduation from high school. A basic limitation is that nobody can benefit from its use financially. That means that if a high school player while still 18 leaves to join a professional or college team, their LL is no longer valid. Further details are covered in the Limited License Agreement.

For clarification, college and MLB players will need to get a license either through their team or directly with us.

This may create a little confusion for coaches. So, let's take care of that now. Once a coach understands the benefits, he/she is allowed to help their young (amateur) players develop their skills of implementation. Knowledgeable hitting coaches will be able to understand the method from what is presented in the book. The *coach's responsibility* is to make sure that any amateur player using the method has a valid amateur Limited License. A coach asking if the player has one is not sufficient. He/she must acquire a copy (proof) of the player's license and keep it on file to avoid personal liability. Getting a Limited License for an amateur player is very easy. Just go to our website www.PivotalSwing.com, pay the fee and the license will be issued.

The above applies to coaches that are *not* earning a salary as a coach. Coaches earning a salary will have to contact us to negotiate a separate licensing agreement.

Enforcement is easy. It is very easy to see if a player is using the Pivotal Swing® method. The characteristics of the method are very distinct. Any reader will know that nobody has in the past or at the time of this publication is using anything like this. The difference in the 'ready position', 'elimination of the stride' and the minimal amount of movement to achieve the 'hitting position' are easily discernible. Utilization of the 'pivotal axis' is also easily recognized. Thus, users of the Pivotal Swing® method will be obvious.

Our objective is to get the Pivotal Swing® method into use. We don't want it to be difficult and have presented a number of paths to do so. We expect the intellectual property (IP) rights to be followed, just as anyone one of you would expect of your IP. As you might expect, violations will be extremely detrimental in wasted time, complexity and costly. Getting a license is very inexpensive compared to dealing with a violation.

Step up to bat! Get a license and let's hit some more line-drives!

END NOTES

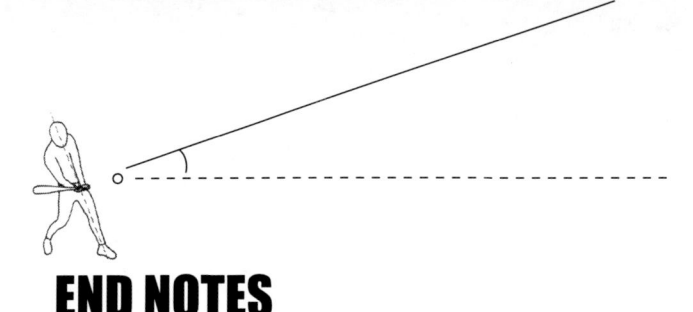

OK, here's the status. In the top of the inning, we hit a home-run. We are moving to the bottom of the last inning. This is the culmination of all the good hits and defensive plays that have gotten us through the 9 innings plus a number of extra innings and we are winning! We have been ahead and, at times we were behind, but battled back. The game is almost over. All we have to do is bring in our 'closer'. The closer's job is to deliver those last 3 outs (with the help of the team) and win the game.

Earlier I told you by reading this book you will never look at the hitting process the same as you did before. To me the status quo is almost never acceptable. The attitude of process improvement (PI) is to constantly be looking at how we can improve all aspects of our daily lives, not only the hitting process. This applies to everyone whether you are a player, coach, influencer (friend, parent, other family members, etc.) or fan. Based on your knowledge and experience, you can find and implement improvements. If you read or get some training on the subject you will get better at doing so.

To me improvement is infectious. Most of my friends get the impact of my application and just understand that's 'me'. So, I'll caution you. Challenging the status quo can be semi-dangerous. You have to keep in mind that others probably aren't as willing to accept being challenged or questioned on why they are following the process the way they have chosen. Tread lightly, especially at first. Give them time to adapt to you and that way of thinking.

The TV show 'Who Wants to be a Millionaire' coined an important question. Is that your final answer? The question is, "is hitting an Art or Science"? I must now ask you, "is that your final answer"? The good news is—you are right (either answer)! Reward yourself! But, just like the TV game, you aren't off the hook, because there are tougher questions. This book has focused on the 'Science' perspective. Does that mean Tony Gwynn is going to come after me with 'both guns-a-blazing'? I doubt it. My reasoning is that

I will bet a huge sum of money that he would have chosen the title of "The Science of Hitting" if Ted William had not already done so. Since I live in San Diego, my proximity has allowed me to follow Tony's career closely. I have not only read his book but have seen him talking to the players at San Diego State University and on TV to others. One of his comments was that he considered himself a 'technician' of the swing. There is a whole lot of science built into that comment. I totally believe that if Tony had ever been introduced to PI tools, he would have developed the Pivotal Swing® and written the book about it.

>>> Game status–Achieved Out #1, and 2 to go

NIH is now up to bat.

'Not Invented Here' (NIH) is a phenomenon in Sony, many other large corporations and whole industries. It pertains to a natural tendency for insiders to reject the ideas and concepts of outsiders. Following a company culture is good. It is probably better to have a company culture that is adept at assessing both inside and outside ideas for their value to the company. Where it comes from should be irrelevant.

My experience with change, change management, company and industry cultures, is that there will be an NIH reaction. Does that change anything? Should I have not written the book because there could be an NIH reaction? Of course that is rhetorical. The book is in front of you. Some folks will receive it with open arms. Some will not. They may have an unconscious reaction to 'who is this outsider' and 'why' should I listen to him? These are typical NIH reactions.

Normal NIH reactions are to question the wrong aspects of the idea, concept, data or method. Often that is done without any true assessment. The best way to make a determination is to fully understand, test and evaluate the inputs to determine acceptance or not. Though I don't expect Tony to come after me with 'both guns-a-blazing', I do expect it from all kinds of critics. They will come from everywhere. I believe I have covered most if not all the answers to the questions they should ask. Answering all the questions they shouldn't ask is wasting both of our time. I don't expect everyone will grasp every detail of the Pivotal Swing® method. There will be a need for additional inputs to those seriously interested in level 2 testing. I will do everything I can to meet those needs.

>>> Game status—Achieved Out #2, and 1 to go

Who should be the last hitter?

Let's choose by deciding 'who will benefit the most'?

By reading this book I can surmise you are at least a fan of the game. This game has brought us endless amounts of enjoyment. Whether you are a player or a fan, there have been many outstanding hits, spectacular defensive plays, closely contested games and championships. Though I view the heavily contested pitching duel as a failure of hitting, I still marvel at the skill and mental tenacity of the players. Even the pitching duel has great memories.

An objective of the book is that we improve the hitting process. Lest I remind you, it is 'we' not I. I have done my part and now you must do yours. There are multiple paths you can follow. It depends on which group you are in.

Players

One option is to implement the Pivotal Swing® and let us know your achievements. There are other options in addition to implementation for you. You can decide to help others as well. As an addition, you can make a determination to learn enough about PI tools that you can make some other improvement to the game.

Coaches

Continue to do your inspiring and developing of the youth entrusted to you on your team. Next to parenting, there is no calling higher than leading youth in the right direction. Their parents have entrusted you to help them find joy in the game while pursuing higher levels of performance and achievement. We all owe a huge debt of gratitude to the long hours you dedicate to these endeavors. Whether you choose to teach them the elements of the Pivotal Swing® method is not your most challenging issue. You know better than most that whether they win or lose, they should enjoy the game and their development. March on!

Family and Friends

You may read this book before the players do. If we are blessed with your approval, you will expose them. Your encouragement to enjoy the game and seek higher levels of performance without destroying the joy is paramount. If I read your hearts correctly, I see some huge emotions tied to that look on your player's face when they produced that 1st hit, home-run or spectacular defensive play. The Pivotal Swing® will produce more of those great moments and add to the joy for all of you.

Fans

This is *'The'* group. All of us are fans! Amen.

All the comments for all the other groups apply to this group. This is who I would choose to go to bat at this stage of the game. Although players are needed, the game is owned by the fans. Baseball team owners and managers know that. Earlier in the book I covered who would benefit the most from the Pivotal Swing® method. Those comments were all directed at players.

The biggest winner of who benefits most is the *'Fans'*! As fans we could be players, coaches, family or friends. We all benefit in some way by an explosion in the amount of hitting. The pitching duel only excites me in one dimension. The added dimensions of increased hitting and exceptional defensive plays in the field, doubles or triples my enjoyment as a fan of the game. More action is equal to more excitement. A better hitting method will produce those added benefits.

This book is not the final step in improving the hitting process. I already know of some additional steps that we can take. Now is not the time. Their time will come in due course. I look forward to working with you on those too.

>>> Game status–Still undecided

I told you my choice for who should be the final hitter, but I didn't hear yours. Until the last hitter comes to the plate, we won't know the outcome of the game.

Everybody loves to win. However, playing the game is one heck of a lot of fun too! Never, never least I emphasize never, not play the game because you might not win. Get your ____ out there and play the game. If you choose to learn and apply PI to the game, more power to you. If the game isn't fun, you missed the point! Have tremendous and exuberant fun in both your achievements and also in finding ways to increase them!!

Your Baseball Friend,
Roger Hart
DPSM

[Note—I'm just messing with you on the DPSM. There is no such designation or credential. It stands for—Developer of the Pivotal Swing® Method. When you become a user of the method, we can designate you as a UPSM or PPSM {User or Practitioner of the Pivotal Swing® Method}. Better yet will be the pros that are leading us into the new .400 hitter era can be designated as MPSM {Master of the Pivotal Swing® Method}.]